Attitudes to punishment: findings from the British Crime Survey

by

Michael Hough
Julian Roberts

A Research and Statistics Directorate Report

Home Office
Research and
Statistics
Directorate

London: Home Office

Home Office Research Studies

The Home Office Research Studies are reports on research undertaken by or on behalf of the Home Office. They cover the range of subjects for which the Home Secretary has responsibility. Titles in the series are listed at the back of this report (copies are available from the address on the back cover). Other publications produced by the Research and Statistics Directorate include Research Findings, the Research Bulletin, Statistical Bulletins and Statistical Papers.

The Research and Statistics Directorate

The Directorate consists of three Units which deal with research and statistics on Crime and Criminal Justice, Offenders and Corrections, Immigration and General Matters; the Programme Development Unit; the Economics Unit; and the Operational Research Unit.

The Research and Statistics Directorate is an integral part of the Home Office, serving the Ministers and the department itself, its services, Parliament and the public through research, development and statistics. Information and knowledge from these sources informs policy development and the management of programmes; their dissemination improves wider public understanding of matters of Home Office concern.

First published 1998

Application for reproduction should be made to the Information and Publications Group, Room 201, Home Office, 50 Queen Anne's Gate, London SW1H 9AT.

Foreword

Those responsible for formulating criminal policy need to have an accurate appreciation of the impact of crime upon society. An important dimension in assessing this is public attitudes to sentencing. Policy needs to command at least a degree of popular consensus; and where this consensus is lacking, it is essential to understand the reasons for it. The British Crime Survey has included questions on attitudes to sentencing since its inception in 1982, and has made a significant contribution to our understanding of the issues. The 1996 sweep covered attitudes to punishment in particular detail, allowing for an in-depth analysis of the topic. This report presents the results of this analysis.

DAVID MOXON
Head of Crime and Criminal Justice Unit
Research and Statistics Directorate

Acknowledgements

We should like to thank Pat Mayhew and Catriona Mirrlees-Black for their consistently helpful advice and suggestions about analysing the British Crime Survey, and for their comments on earlier drafts of this report. We are also grateful to the Home Office for funding this study.

MICHAEL HOUGH
JULIAN ROBERTS

Contents

Summary

The British Crime Survey (BCS) has been an important source of information about attitudes to punishment in England and Wales since it was set up in 1982. This report presents findings mainly from the most recent sweep, carried out in 1996. This had a nationally representative core sample of 16,348 respondents aged 16 or over, with a response rate of 83 per cent. One part of the interview was devoted specifically to sentencing issues. Roughly half the sample were asked a series of questions covering:

- their knowledge of crime and sentencing

- their assessments of sentencers and sentences

- the sentence which they thought should be passed in a specific case of burglary

- their views on the best ways of tackling crime

Those identified by the survey as victims have been asked since 1984 what punishment they thought their offender should get. Results for victims of burglary and car theft are presented here.

Knowledge of crime and sentencing

The 1996 BCS found widespread ignorance amongst the public in England and Wales about crime and criminal justice statistics. Misperceptions were systematic rather than random, in that majorities overestimated the gravity of crime problems, and underestimated the severity of the criminal justice system. Findings of particular interest are:

- the mistaken belief amongst the majority that recorded crime had rapidly increased

- substantial overestimates of the proportion of recorded crime involving violence

- a tendency to underestimate the proportion of the population with criminal records

- large minorities being unaware of the upward trend in the use of imprisonment

- widespread ignorance of sentences available to the court

- very substantial underestimates of the courts' use of imprisonment for three types of crime – rape, mugging and burglary.

Assessments of sentencers and sentences

The survey shows that the public in England and Wales take a jaundiced view of sentencers and sentencing. Eighty-two per cent of the sample thought that judges were out of touch with the public; the figure for magistrates was 63 per cent. Four-fifths of people think that sentences are too lenient, half saying that they are much too lenient. Judges were thought to be doing the worst job amongst criminal justice professionals. The order of the ratings of these groups, from top to bottom, was:

- the police service

- the Prison Service

- magistrates

- the Crown Prosecution Service

- the probation service

- judges.

The BCS has demonstrated equally clearly, however, that at least in part, public dissatisfaction is grounded in ignorance of current practice, and in ignorance of current crime trends. Those who were most dissatisfied were most likely to overestimate the growth in crime and the degree to which crime is violent, underestimate the courts' use of imprisonment and underestimate the clear-up rate.

Those who were most likely to underestimate the courts' use of imprisonment have lower educational attainment than others, were likely to be above average age and were more likely to read tabloid newspapers. Women were more likely than men to underestimate the proportion of convicted rapists sent to prison, and owner occupiers more likely than others to underestimate the use of imprisonment for burglars.

When people were asked about a real case of burglary, their sentencing prescriptions were, on balance, well in line with current sentencing practice. They were told that the burglary was committed in daytime by someone with previous convictions, and involved the theft of a video and television set from the home of an elderly man who was out at the time. Fifty-four per cent of the sample wanted a prison sentence, with sentence lengths averaging less than the two years that the burglar actually got. The remainder of the sample proposed community service orders (26%), a fine (21%), a suspended sentence (18%), tagging (11%) or probation (9%). A large minority (44%) suggested compensation, either by itself or in combination with imprisonment or another penalty. Those who had been victims of crime were no more punitive than others; this held true for victims of burglary as well as for victims of other types of crime.

The survey included an experiment to see if people's preference for imprisonment was a function of their ignorance of the alternatives. Whilst most of the sample selected their preferred sentences from a 'menu' on a showcard, a sub-sample were denied this, having to make 'top of the head' choices instead. This group was much less inclined to select community penalties and compensation, and more inclined to select imprisonment – 67 per cent against 54 per cent. The finding underscores how sentencing preferences are shaped by the level of information available to respondents.

The best ways of tackling crime

Most of the sample thought that many different factors underlie current levels of crime. They believed that sentencing levels were an important determinant of crime trends. However, they tended to see changes in parenting and in unemployment levels as more promising ways of reducing crime. Their attitudes towards greater use of imprisonment was at least ambivalent, with a widespread belief that imprisonment can stimulate as well as prevent further crime. Far more people expressed a preference for tougher community penalties (56%) than for building new prisons (18%) as a means of tackling prison overcrowding.

Victims' sentencing preferences

The BCS shows that there was a marked increase over the period from 1984 to 1996 in victims' preference for tough sentencing, at least in relation to two types of crime, burglary and car theft. There was no evidence to suggest that this trend was a function simply of increasing seriousness of the average crime of this sort. Nor was there any evidence that the experience of victimisation fuels a desire for tougher penalties. Victims' preferences did not seem, on balance, to be substantially out of line with current sentencing practice.

Policy implications

The 1996 BCS suggests that there is a crisis of confidence in sentencers which needs tackling with some urgency. People think that sentencers are out of touch, and that their sentences are far too soft.

A criminal policy of 'playing to the gallery' and extending the use of imprisonment further is not appropriate. The BCS suggests an ingrained belief in lenient sentences whatever the reality – the same way that they probably assume prices are rising, regardless of the actual rate of inflation. The most likely reason for this is that people receive information about sentencing largely from the media, and media news values militate against balanced coverage. Erratic court sentences make news, and sensible ones do not. As a result large segments of the population are exposed to a steady stream of unrepresentative stories about sentencing incompetence.

Correcting public misperception about sentencing trends in this country should promote greater public confidence in judges and magistrates. And, since the judiciary occupy such a critical place in the criminal justice system, increasing confidence in the courts should promote confidence in the administration of justice.

Improving public understanding of sentencing and crime is easier said than done. A great deal has already been done to improve the quality and accessibility of crime and sentencing statistics. However there remains obvious room for improvement. The most challenging demands are in identifying effective ways of interrupting the processes which feed public cynicism. To date very limited use has been made of the communication techniques of the late twentieth century in letting the public know about current sentencing practice. A successful strategy for tackling public misperceptions will almost certainly have to resort to these techniques. It will have to identify key audiences, such as opinion formers, victims, potential offenders and people at risk of offending, and convey appropriately to each audience an accurate portrayal of current sentencing practice.

I Introduction

Of all criminal justice issues, sentencing is perhaps the most controversial, and the one which attracts the greatest degree of public concern. The public tend to be more critical of sentencers than any other decision-makers in the criminal justice process (cf Walker and Hough, 1988; Roberts, 1992). Research in several countries has shown that public support for the police is highest, while the heaviest criticisms are reserved for judges.[1] Whilst it is obviously important to maintain public confidence throughout the criminal process, it is, therefore, a particular issue in relation to the judiciary.

The need to sustain public confidence means that public opinion plays an important, albeit indirect role in sentencing policy and practice. Most recently, the Lord Chief Justice, Lord Bingham (1997) observed that he did not "consider it would be right, even if it were possible, for judges to ignore the opinion of the public". He continued by noting that "the increase in the prison population is not explained by any recent increase in sentencing powers, and I have no doubt that it is related to the pressure of public opinion". Politicians, too, have frequently referred to the need to reflect or incorporate the views of the public in the debate surrounding sentencing policy (see Ashworth and Hough, 1996, for further discussion).

Whatever the precise nature of the linkage between opinion and sentencing practice, therefore, it is obvious that those who are responsible for sentencing policy require a good understanding of what people know and think about sentencing. The difficulty is that public opinion manifests itself to sentencers and policymakers in many different ways. Most obviously, the media - and the tabloid press in particular – simultaneously reflect and shape knowledge and opinion. There are politicians' postbags, and the activities of formal and informal pressure groups. However, these conduits of public opinion can provide a distorted image of public views. The only truly valid measure of opinion is a representative survey. Even with such a survey, however, problems remain. Researchers must ensure that the questions posed to the public are adequate to capture the complexities of the sentencing process. As we shall demonstrate below, simply asking the public whether they think sentences are too harsh or too lenient is an inadequate and indeed misleading way of measuring public opinion.

---

1   Huang and Vaughn (1996) summarise research in America which shows very positive attitudes to the police. For example, a recent American survey found that three-quarters of respondents rated the police as "excellent". Similar results emerge in Canada (Roberts and Stalans, 1997).

Certainly, simple survey questions of this sort paint a clear picture of a punitive public. For example, questions along the line *"Are sentences too harsh, too lenient or about right?"* find large majorities saying the sentences are not harsh enough.[2] A poll carried out for the Daily Mail (1 April 1996) found 92 per cent of a random sample supporting "tougher sentences for criminals, especially persistent criminals".[3] Findings of this sort have done much to consolidate the view amongst politicians and criminal justice professionals that the public wants tougher justice. However, this is a serious oversimplification of public attitudes to sentencing.

Survey research conducted in the 1980s (Hough and Moxon, 1985; Walker and Hough, 1988) suggests a more qualified interpretation of public opinion about sentencing. This work indicated that the public were less punitive than was generally supposed. When asked about the appropriate punishments for individual crimes, many people's preferences tended to reflect the range of sentences actually imposed by the courts. This finding has been replicated in several other countries such as Australia, Canada, The Netherlands and the United States (see Diamond and Stalans, 1989; Walker and Hough, 1988; Roberts and Stalans, 1997; Walker, Collins and Wilson, 1988).

Clearly though, the public are dissatisfied with sentencing practice, or what they perceive sentencing practice to be. What is responsible for this dissatisfaction? One explanation is that people simply do not have an accurate perception of the sentencing process. Recent qualitative work employing focus groups (see Hough, 1996) has uncovered systematic ignorance of current sentencing patterns, and has demonstrated that this is a factor fuelling public dissatisfaction with the courts.[4]

Information, it would appear, is critical to public attitudes to sentencing. As a general rule, the less information that people have about any specific case, the more likely they are to advocate a punitive response to it. This was demonstrated by a Canadian study which divided a sample of respondents in half. One half were given a relatively brief newspaper account of the sentencing decision in an assault case. Most people who read this account of the case thought that the sentence was too lenient. The other group were given a complete summary of all the court documents. In other words, they had the same amount of information at their disposal as the judge in the case. Only a small minority (19%) of this group believed that the sentence was too lenient (Doob and Roberts, 1988). This experiment demonstrated

---

2   Similar results emerge with general questions relating to capital punishment. Three-quarters of the public favour re-introduction of the death penalty (see Jowell et al., 1994).

3   One can speculate that questions using less loaded terms – 'repeat offenders' or 'law-breaker' rather than 'persistent criminals' – might have generated less consensus.

4   Research in America, Australia, and Canada has also found that the public have little idea of sentencing patterns or statutory maxima (see Williams, Gibbs and Erickson, 1980; Indermaur, 1987; Canadian Sentencing Commission, 1987).

that the amount of information about a case is critical in determining public reaction. Unfortunately, most newspaper descriptions of a case provide very little information. As well, the cases chosen for coverage by newspapers tend to be ones that resulted in what appears to be a lenient sentence. Both these trends contribute to encouraging a public perception that the system is very lenient, and that judges are thoroughly out of touch with the views of the community.

One weakness of Doob and Roberts' experiment (and with other studies that have adopted this research strategy) is that the subjects were people who had been recruited for a social science study. This kind of sample, it can be argued, is not representative of the general population. A survey carried out in England for the Royal Commission on Criminal Justice (Zander and Henderson, 1993) cannot be criticised on the same grounds. The survey interviewed actual jurors and came to similar conclusions. Participants were asked what they thought of the sentence that had been imposed in the case in which they had served as jurors. Fewer than one juror in four thought that the sentence imposed was less severe than they had expected.

Finally, the critical role of information in determining attitudes also emerges from US research on attitudes towards the use of imprisonment (Doble and Klein, 1989; English, Crouch and Pullen, 1989). In these studies, people were asked to sentence an offender described in a brief scenario. Half the sample were given no other information about the possible sentences that could be imposed; in other words they correspond to the average person on the street. The other half were given a complete list of the range of community-based penalties available to, and used by, the courts. People who were given the complete list of available penalties were less likely than members of the other group to advocate imprisonment of the offender. The lesson is clear: part of the reason why so many people support the use of imprisonment is that they may simply be unaware that there are other ways of punishing offenders. In other words, the public may not be implacably opposed to alternative punishments – but simply be ill-informed about them.

While these studies call into question stereotypes of a public committed to "hang'em and flog'em" sentencing, many were mounted abroad, and many are now quite old. The 1996 British Crime Survey offered a timely opportunity both to chart opinion in an authoritative way and to explore the factors which shape this opinion.

The British Crime Survey

The British Crime Survey (BCS) has been an important source of information about attitudes to punishment in England and Wales,[5] since it was set up in 1982. This report presents findings mainly from the most recent sweep, carried out in 1996. Details about BCS methodology are given in Appendix A. The 1996 BCS had a nationally representative core sample of 16,348 respondents aged 16 or over. The response rate was 83 per cent.

The 1996 version of the BCS contained a module devoted specifically to sentencing issues. Roughly half the sample (8,365 respondents) were asked a series of questions about various aspects of the sentencing process. In addition to the standard question about sentence severity *("Are the sentences handed down by the courts too tough, about right or too lenient?")*, respondents were asked to provide a sentence for a specific case. Previous research in the United Kingdom and elsewhere has shown that it is important to provide a specific case scenario in order to ensure that respondents are not thinking of an atypical case. When respondents are asked to respond to the general question without a specific case, they tend to think of the most serious crime committed by an offender with a long criminal record (c.f. Doob and Roberts, 1988).

The 1996 BCS also contained a series of questions which evaluated respondents' *knowledge* of the sentencing and conditional release process. For example, respondents were asked to estimate the incarceration rate for three common offences. After stating the percentage of offenders convicted of these crimes that they thought were imprisoned, respondents were asked to give their opinion about the percentage that they believed *should* be incarcerated. In this way, analyses can relate what the public think about sentencing trends to public opinion about sentencing practices. As well, respondents were asked a series of questions about related issues such as crime prevention, prison conditions and prison overcrowding. Finally, they were asked to evaluate a number of criminal justice professions, including the police, the Crown Prosecution service, judges and magistrates.

Outline of the report

Chapter 2 summarises findings from questions which probed public *knowledge* of the criminal justice system. In Chapter 3 we focus on *opinion* regarding the sentencing process. We first examine general ratings of sentencers and sentencing; we then examine how the ratings (largely negative) correlate with misperceptions about the criminal process; and finally, we examine the sentencing preferences expressed in response to

---

5   The 1996 Scottish Crime Survey (MVA, 1997) has also covered attitudes towards crime and the criminal process, though not in a form which is comparable to the findings presented here.

specific cases. Chapter 4 presents findings about somewhat wider questions on crime control strategy, and Chapter 5 discusses attitudes to punishment amongst victims, including findings on trends since 1984. Chapter 6 summarises the findings and draws out policy implications. Wherever possible, we compare and contrast the present findings with the results of research from other countries, in order to view British attitudes in context. As we shall see, many findings are consistent with research elsewhere. Appendix A contains additional information on the methodology of the British Crime Survey. That part of the questionnaire which dealt with attitudes to punishment can be found in Appendix B.

2 Knowledge of crime and criminal justice

This chapter presents findings from the 1996 BCS on public knowledge about crime and criminal justice. Respondents were asked about:

- national crime trends

- the proportion of recorded crime involving violence

- the annual number of murders in England and Wales

- the clear-up rate

- the proportion of the male population with criminal records

- changes in the use of imprisonment

- the range of sentences available to the court

- current sentencing practice in the use of imprisonment for three crimes

- time served in prison.

National crime rates

Respondents were asked whether the *recorded* crime rate for the country as a whole had changed over the previous two years (i.e., 1993–1995). The number of recorded crimes in 1995 was eight per cent lower than in 1993 (Povey, Prime and Taylor, 1997). As this information had not been published at the time of fieldwork, people could not have known it. However, crime figures for England and Wales are published every six months, and the previous three sets all showed significant falls; figures for the 12 months ending June 1995 were ten per cent lower than two years earlier (Home Office, 1995).

Figure 2.1 gives a breakdown of responses (excluding the one per cent who did not express a view). It shows that three-quarters of the sample "got it wrong". Thus well-publicised statistics about falling crime had very little impact on popular perceptions – a finding in keeping with surveys in other western nations (see Doble, 1996; Roberts and Stalans, 1997, for a review).

Both this and previous sweeps of the BCS asked respondents about changes in the crime rate in their area. Whilst three-quarters thought that there was more crime nationally, just over half (54%) thought that crime *in their area* had increased. This proportion was higher in 1994 at 64 per cent and higher still at 67 per cent in 1992 (Mirrlees-Black et al., 1996).

Figure 2.1 Changes in recorded crime

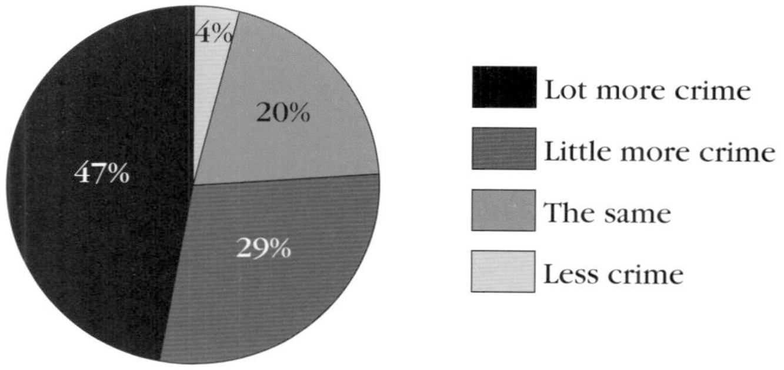

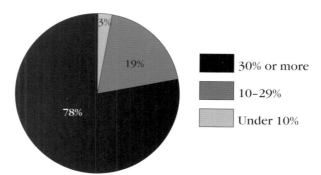

Question: Would you say that there is more (recorded) crime, less crime or about the same amount since two years ago?

Figure 2.2 How much crime is violent?

Question: Of every 100 crimes recorded by the police, what number do you think involve violence or the threat of violence?

There are several possible reasons why people disbelieve or fail to attend to published crime statistics. First, headlines such as "Crime rate soars" have been such a staple of tabloid journalism for so long that it would probably take years of falling crime rates before the change became embedded in public consciousness. Second, large proportions of the population will simply miss or forget relevant newspaper stories and broadcasts. Third, even when national crime rates fall, local crime rates may have risen; and respondents in such areas would reasonably extrapolate from the local experience in answering questions about national crime rates. Finally the police figures probably were an unreliable guide to trends over this period. The BCS provides a better measure for crimes against individuals and their private property; the 1996 sweep actually showed a four per cent *rise* between 1993 and 1995 (Mirrlees-Black et al., 1996). But even if we use the BCS as a yardstick, almost half (46%) of the sample were wrong in saying that there was "a lot more crime" nationally than two years before.

Perceptions of violent crime

Research in other countries has shown that violence is central to public conceptions of crime. One explanation for this is that the news media – which constitute the public's primary source of information about crime – disproportionately report crimes of violence. The more lurid and horrific, the more newsworthy the crime. In fact, around six per cent of crimes recorded by the police in England and Wales at the time of the survey were violent or sexual in nature (Barclay, 1995); if BCS figures are used, woundings and robbery again account for 6%; a further 15 per cent are common assaults involving little or no injury. Figure 2.2 shows that the public substantially overestimates the extent to which crimes involve violence. Excluding the three per cent who chose "don't know" as a response,[1] almost four out of five said that 30 per cent or more of crimes were violent.[2] The mean response was 50 per cent.

---

1   This in itself is interesting. It suggests that people are confident that their perceptions of criminal justice are accurate.

2   Comparable trends emerge in other countries. When this same question was posed in Canada, three-quarters of Canadians estimated the same statistic to lie between 30 and 100 per cent (Doob and Roberts, 1988). Indermaur (1990) reports the same finding using a sample of Australian respondents.

3   Mitchell (forthcoming) has shown that the public is sensitive to the wide variation in gravity of offences of homicide – but it is unlikely that public conceptions of what constitutes murder are fully consistent with legal ones. In responding to this question, people may have a rather different, broader definition in their minds.

Murders in England and Wales

Respondents were asked to estimate the number of murders recorded in England and Wales in 1995. Comparing public perceptions to reality is a little complex. Police statistics classify killings as homicides, making no distinction between murder and manslaughter. In the large number of cases involving prosecution and conviction, the court's verdict subsequently enables a distinction to be made between murder and manslaughter. In 1995, the police recorded 754 homicides; and extrapolating from cases which actually came to court, between 350 and 400 could be regarded as murders.[3]

People had more difficulty with this question than any other. This is reflected in the relatively large number of people who refused to respond or who chose "don't know" as a response: over five per cent. When they did respond, people chose a wide range of responses, many of which were clearly guesses. Fully one-quarter of the sample estimated under 50, while 3 per cent estimated in excess of 3,000. The average response to this question was 616. It would be stretching things to conclude that the British public tends to over-estimate the number of murders – a finding which *has* been established in North America (Roberts, 1992).

Crimes cleared up by the police

An important indicator of police performance is the percentage of crime incidents that are cleared up.[4] The most relevant statistics, covering 1995 show a clear-up rate of 26 per cent (Home Office, 1996). The clear-up rate receives little publicity in the news media, at least relative to trends in recorded crime. Accordingly, it would be unsurprising if most members of the public had little accurate idea of this statistic – or even, in many cases, an understanding of the concept. People were asked the following question: *"Crimes are recorded as **cleared up** by the police when the offender is prosecuted or otherwise admits guilt. Out of every 100 crimes reported to the police, what number do you think are 'cleared up'?"* Respondents' estimates varied from zero to 100 per cent. Table 2.1 shows the results.

---

4   Crimes are regarded as cleared up if they result in one of the following: a charge; a summons; a caution; a request by the offender that the offence be 'taken into consideration' by the courts when sentencing for another crime; or a formal admission of guilt made whilst serving a prison sentence for another offence.

Table 2:1 Estimates of the clear-up rate

Percentage of the sample making .....

	%
Underestimates (under 20% cleared up)	9
Accurate estimates (20–30% cleared up)	26
Overestimates (31% or more cleared up)	65
Total	*100*

One interpretation of this pattern of results suggests that most respondents had little idea about the actual clearance rate, and were simply guessing. Certainly, the response most frequently chosen (by one in five respondents) was 50 per cent – the successful bluffer's way of expressing ignorance. However, people who overestimate clear-up rates also tend to rate the police most favourably. Thus overestimating clear-up rates could equally well be interpreted either as an expression of confidence in the police, or as one of the factors which actually shapes this level of confidence. We shall return to this issue later in the report.

Percentage of adult males with criminal records

By the time that they reach the age of 40, fully 40 per cent of men in Britain have a criminal record for a non-motoring offence – a fact little known among the general public. When they were asked to estimate the percentage of 40-year-old men with a criminal record, almost two-thirds under-estimated this statistic. The median response was 30 per cent. If we consider a response between 35 per cent and 45 per cent to be correct, one in seven (14%) got it right. Over half (56%) under-estimated the statistic, while 30 per cent overestimated.

One interpretation of this pattern of results relates to public perceptions of criminality. Other research has demonstrated that the public believe that crime is committed by a small, easily identifiable population of repeat offenders. This belief leads the majority of people to under-estimate the number of men with criminal records.

Changes in courts' use of imprisonment

Respondents were asked if they thought that the proportion of offenders sent to prison had increased, decreased or stayed the same over the previous two years. The correct answer is that there was a very substantial increase in the custodial population and a corresponding reduction in the community penalties. The number of persons sentenced to custody rose from 58,400 in 1993 to 79,100 in 1995, an increase of 35 per cent (Home Office, 1996); the proportion of convicted offenders sent to prison rose from 15 per cent to 20 per cent.

Just over half the sample (56%) were aware of this change. Roughly a quarter (27%) believed there had been no change while 15 per cent believed that there had been a fall (the remaining 2 per cent said they did not know or refused to answer). Widespread news media coverage of the swelling prison population must account for this finding.

Knowledge of sentencing options

One question explored public knowledge of sentencing alternatives. Taking for granted that everyone is aware of imprisonment, respondents were asked to list sentencing options other than imprisonment. The thinking behind the question was that public enthusiasm for imprisonment might at least in part reflect ignorance of the alternatives.

The results indicated widespread awareness of some, but by no means all, non-custodial sentences. Over two-thirds (69%) of respondents identified community service; this was the most widely-known sentencing option. Over half (58%) identified a fine. Surprisingly perhaps, only about a third (35%) of the sample identified probation. Even smaller percentages of respondents were aware of the other alternatives: suspended sentence[5] (30%); compensation (16%); conditional discharge (8%); electronic tagging (7%). It is clear then, that although large percentages of the public are aware of some community penalties (such as community service), others such as probation are not at all salient in people's minds when thinking about sentencing.

---

[5] This sentence now accounts for only one per cent of the total – though it continues to loom large in public consciousness (see Hough, 1996).

The use of imprisonment for specific offences

A final set of questions testing knowledge of the criminal justice system concerned sentencing for three familiar crimes: rape, mugging and residential burglary. For each of these offences, respondents were asked what percentage of convictions for males, aged 21 and over, actually result in custody. In our analysis of these data, we have classified respondents into various categories, reflecting their degree of accuracy in estimating the incarceration rate for these crimes. We have regarded estimates as correct if they fell roughly within ten per cent of the right answer. Those whose estimates were roughly 10–30 per cent too low were classified as "a bit too low". For example, for residential burglary, the "correct" answer to the question of what percentage of offenders were imprisoned in 1995 is 61 per cent; any respondent providing an estimate between 50 per cent and 69 per cent was classified as being accurate,[6] and those scoring between 31% and 49% were classified as "a bit too low". Figure 2.3 and Table 2.2 summarise the findings.

Large majorities of respondents settled for estimates of current imprisonment rates which were much too low for all three types of crime. For rape, 97 per cent of adult males convicted in 1995 were sent to prison (data supplied by Home Office RSD). Respondents' median estimate was 50 per cent. Figure 2.3 classifies 18 per cent of respondents as accurate, in that they estimated between 85 per cent and 100 per cent. Twenty-six per cent were 'a bit low', settling for between 60 per cent and 84 per cent. The remaining 57 per cent made estimates which were 'much too low'.

Since there is no legal offence of mugging, the survey defined it as *"theft in the street by means of force or the threat of force"*. The Home Office cannot provide sentencing statistics for this sub-group of robberies. However, they probably make up the bulk of convictions, with robberies in banks, shops and other businesses being relatively rare. Almost all (92%) of adult male offenders convicted in 1995 of any form of robbery were imprisoned. We have conservatively estimated that the percentage of convicted adult muggers who get custodial sentences is in the region of 70 per cent. According to this yardstick, 12 per cent of respondents were accurate, and five per cent over-estimated the imprisonment rate, providing estimates between 80 per cent and 100 per cent. Once again however, the vast majority of the sample (75%) under-estimated the severity of sentencing trends. Twenty per cent made a small underestimate – between 45 per cent and 59 per cent, and 62 per cent made larger underestimates. The median estimate of the percentage of adult muggers sent to prison was 35 per cent.

---

6   Classification decisions were not made rigidly in accordance with these criteria. For example, we erred on the side of caution by including as accurate the large numbers who said that 50 per cent of convicted burglars were imprisoned. Strictly speaking our criteria imply that these were "a bit low".

Figure 2.3: Knowledge of sentencing practice: estimates of courts' use of custody

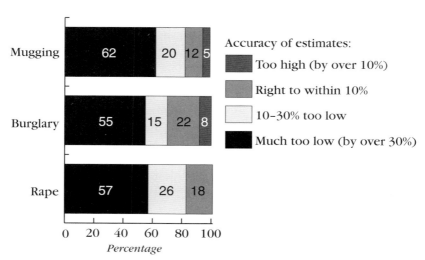

Question: Out of every 100 men aged 21 or over who are convicted of [rape/mugging/house burglary] how many do you think are sent to prison?

For residential burglary, 61 per cent of convicted adult male house-burglars were imprisoned in 1995. Twenty-two per cent of responses were classified as "correct", namely those falling between 50 and 69 per cent. A further eight per cent provided an over-estimate. Once again, the majority of the sample under-estimated the severity of the system; 15 per cent were 'a bit low' (31–49%) and the remaining 55 per cent made grosser underestimates. The median estimate was 30 per cent.

Not surprisingly, responses to the three questions were inter-correlated. That is, people who under-estimated the proportion of rapists sent to prison also under-estimated the percentage of muggers and burglars who were imprisoned.

Table 2.2: Summary of public estimates of imprisonment rates

	Rape	Mugging	Burglary
Over-estimate Rape: not applicable Mugging: 80–100% Burglary: 70–100%	–	5%	8%
Accurate Rape: 85–100% Mugging: 60–79% Burglary: 50–69%	18%	12%	22%
Small under-estimate Rape: 60–85% Mugging: 45–59% Burglary: 31–49%	26%	20%	15%
Large under-estimate Rape: 0–59% Mugging: 0–44% Burglary: 0–30%	57%	62%	55%
Total	100%	100%	100%

Question: *Out of every 100 men aged 21 or over who are convicted of rape (mugging/ house burglary), how many do you think are sent to prison?*

After estimating actual imprisonment rates, respondents were asked to say what proportion *should* be imprisoned. Responses were unambiguous with respect to rapists. The mean was 94 per cent, and over four-fifths of the sample said that all rapists should be imprisoned. For muggers, the mean was 84 per cent, with 57 per cent saying that all muggers should be imprisoned. For burglars the mean was 80 per cent, with less than half of the sample (42%) saying that all adult burglars should go to prison. The implications of these findings are discussed in Chapter 3.

Estimates of average time served in prison

Respondents were asked the following specific question: *"If someone is sentenced to serve 12 months [in prison], how long, on average do you think they will actually spend in prison?".* The right answer is six months (assuming that no significant amount of extra time was awarded as a result of infractions of prison rules). In general, people were fairly accurate. Half (49%) put the figure at five to seven months. One in six (17%) underestimated, and a third overestimated. The median estimate of the time served was actually six months.

Summary

These findings demonstrate very clearly that there is widespread ignorance about crime and criminal justice statistics. Misperceptions seem systematic rather than random, in that majorities overestimated the gravity of crime problems, and underestimated the severity of the criminal justice system. Findings of particular interest were:

- the mistaken belief amongst the majority that crime was rapidly increasing

- substantial overestimates of the proportion of recorded crime involving violence

- a tendency to underestimate the proportion of the population with criminal records

- large minorities being unaware of the upward trend in the use of imprisonment

- widespread ignorance of sentences available to the court

- substantial underestimates of the use of imprisonment for three types of crime.

3 Opinion about sentencers and sentencing

The first part of this chapter presents results on assessments of sentencers' performance and abilities. As will emerge, the results confirm earlier work suggesting widespread dissatisfaction (e.g., Walker and Hough, 1988; Hough, 1996). The middle part of the chapter explores the relationship between this dissatisfaction and public misperceptions about crime and sentencing. The chapter ends with an examination of the sorts of sentences which people think ought to be passed in specific cases.

Assessments of sentencers' performance

The 1996 BCS shows that the majority of the public have little regard for sentencers' performance. Respondents were asked several relevant questions:

- whether sentences were tough enough

- whether judges and magistrates were in touch with ordinary people

- whether judges and magistrates were doing a good job.

Figure 3.1 shows that four out of five respondents thought sentences were too lenient to some degree (excluding the 2% who expressed no opinion). Half said that sentences were "much too lenient". This result is consistent with similar research in other common law countries.[1] There is more public consensus on this issue than any other in criminal justice, including the death penalty.

As Figure 3.2 shows, people also thought that sentencers were out of touch. More than four out of five thought judges were out of touch to some degree, and 46 per cent thought they were very out of touch. Magistrates fared better: only 21 per cent of the sample viewed them as being very out of touch. Even so, almost two-thirds thought they were out of touch to some degree.

---

1   For example, 80 per cent of the Canadian public and a similar percentage of Americans hold this view, and have done so for over 30 years (e.g., Flanagan and Longmire, 1996).

Figure 3.1: Are sentences tough enough?

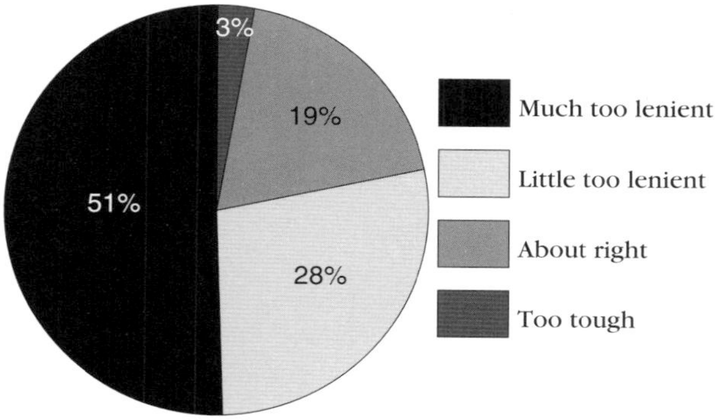

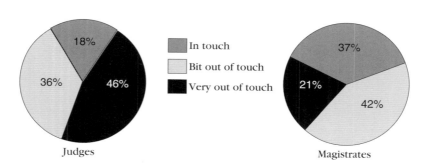

Much too lenient

Little too lenient

About right

Too tough

Question: In general, would you say that sentences handed down by the courts are too tough, about right or too lenient?

Figure 3.2: Are sentencers in touch?

In touch

Bit out of touch

Very out of touch

Judges

Magistrates

Question: Do you think that [judges/magistrates] are generally in touch or out of touch with what ordinary people think?

Figure 3.3 compares the ratings of the job done by judges and magistrates with those of other professionals. Judges emerge with the lowest ratings of all seven groups: excluding "don't knows", 32 per cent thought they did a poor job, 49 per cent a fair job, and 20 per cent thought they did a good job. Magistrates do marginally better than the probation service and the CPS, but not as well as the prison or police services.[2]

Taken together, these findings suggest that sentencers, and judges in particular, face a crisis of public confidence. Their sentences are widely regarded as far too lenient; they are reckoned to be out of touch with ordinary people; and they are thought to do a worse job than the police, the CPS or prison services.

Public ratings of sentencers and public misperceptions

In devising a policy response to public dissatisfaction with sentencers, the first step must be to identify its source. If public attitudes are grounded in misperceptions, then the problem is one of communication. But if the better-informed members of society are equally dissatisfied, this would point to a more substantive mismatch, soluble either by persuading people of the merits of current practice, or else by adjusting practice.

Figure 3.3: How good a job are they doing? Sentencers and other justice agencies

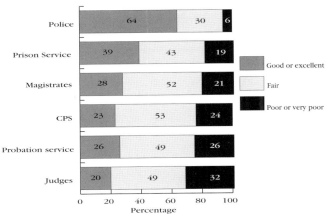

Question: We would like to know how good a job you think each of these groups of people are doing? How good a job are the [police etc.] doing? Would that be an excellent, good, fair, poor or very poor job

---

2   The police findings are consistent with other questions in the BCS about the quality of local policing. Eighty-one per cent of respondents in the 1996 BCS thought that the police in their area did a good job (Mirrlees-Black and Budd, 1997).

As a first step in our analysis, we checked that the view that sentencers were out of touch and did a poor job was indeed associated with a belief that they were too lenient. Tables 3.1 and 3.2 confirm this to be so for judges: the more that people thought sentences too lenient, the more likely they were to believe that judges were out of touch with society, and doing a poor job. Very similar findings emerged in relation to magistrates. This suggests that when people express the view that judges are out of touch, they specifically mean with respect to the leniency of sentences that are imposed.

Table 3.1 Perceptions of whether judges are in touch and attitudes towards sentence severity

Judges are:			
	In touch	A bit out of touch	Very out of touch
Sentences are:	%	%	%
Too tough	2	2	3
About right	42	22	7
Too lenient	57	76	90
	100	100	100

Table 3.2 Perceptions of how good a job judges do and attitudes towards sentence severity

The job that judges are doing is:			
	Good	Fair	Poor
Sentences are:	%	%	%
Too tough	3	2	3
About right	36	20	6
Too lenient	61	78	92
	100	100	100

Having established that the belief in sentencers' leniency is implicated in public dissatisfaction, we then examined how the belief in leniency correlated with misperceptions about sentencing practice. Table 3.3 crosstabulates belief about leniency with estimates of the use of imprisonment for rapists, muggers and burglars. For all three crime types, the lower the estimated use of imprisonment, the greater the belief that sentencers were too lenient. For example, people who believed that sentences were too lenient generated a lower average estimate of the percentage of rapists incarcerated than did people who believed that sentences were about right. This implies that people who are dissatisfied with the severity of sentences are also those who are particularly inaccurate.

Table 3.3 Estimates of imprisonment rates and beliefs about sentence severity

	Average estimates of imprisonment rate:		
	Rape	Mugging	Burglary
Sentences are:			
Much too lenient	50%	34%	31%
About right	54%	38%	35%
Too lenient	60%	43%	39%

Averaging the estimates of imprisonment rates for the three crimes shows the contrast between respondents who believe sentences are much too lenient and the rest of the sample. Averaged across the offences, respondents who felt sentences are much too lenient believed that 38 per cent of offenders were incarcerated. The average for those who felt that sentences were a little too lenient was 42 per cent, and those who thought that sentences were about right or too tough generated an average of 47 per cent. This suggests that ignorance about current practice is one source of public dissatisfaction with sentencing.

If beliefs about leniency correlated with misperceptions about sentencing practice, they also were related to misperceptions of the crime rate, as Table 3.4 shows. People who thought that crime was steeply on the increase were more likely than others to think that sentences were too lenient.

Table 3.4 Perceptions of crime rate and attitudes towards sentence severity

National crime trends:			
	Rising a lot	Rising a bit	Stable or falling
Sentences are:	%	%	%
Too tough	2	2	4
About right	11	21	29
Too lenient	88	77	67
	100	100	100

We can pursue this issue more directly by relating evaluations of judges to the question in which respondents were asked whether they thought that sentencing has played a role in the increasing crime rate. Not surprisingly, people who thought that sentencing had been a significant cause of changes in the crime rate were significantly more negative in their evaluations of judges. Thus of those respondents who felt that sentencing has been the most important cause of crime, almost half also felt that judges had been doing a poor or very poor job. In contrast, of those who saw no relationship between sentencing patterns and changes in the crime rate, only 24 per cent felt that judges were doing a poor or very poor job (see Table 3.5).

Table 3:5 Ratings of judges and views about impact of sentencing on crime

	How good a job are judges doing:		
Sentencing has been....	Excellent/ good	Fair	Poor/very poor
The most important cause	12%	41%	46%
A major cause	17%	49%	34%
Only a minor cause	25%	53%	22%
Not a cause	28%	49%	24%

....of changes in the crime rate

These trends also support the interpretation that the public regard judges as playing an important role in crime control. People tend to think that varying the severity of penalties will have an impact on crime rates; more lenient sentences will lead to higher crime rates, harsher to a fall in crime. Here too, there are international parallels.[3]

We carried out a logistic regression analysis to assess which aspects of public misperception were most closely associated with a belief that sentences were far too soft. Seven variables were included in the analysis. One, the estimated proportion of convicted rapists who are sent to prison, was rejected as a statistically non-significant predictor. The remaining six were all identified as statistically signifiant predictors, and are listed below, in order of predictiveness:[4]

1. Changes in national crime rate
    (Those saying "a lot more crime" were most likely to think sentences far too soft.)

2. Changes in use of imprisonment
    (Those saying prison use "the same/down" were most likely to say sentences far too soft.)

3. Estimated number of convicted muggers who were sent to prison
    (Under-estimators were most likely to say sentences were far too soft.)

4. The proportion of recorded crime involving violence
    (Over-estimators were most likely to say sentences were far too soft.)

5. Estimated number of convicted burglars who were sent to prison
    (Under-estimators were most likely to say sentences were far too soft.)

6. Estimates of the clear-up rate
    (Under-estimators were most likely to say sentences were far too soft.)

This analysis provides strong evidence that people's dissatisfaction with perceived sentencing lenience stems at least in part from misperceptions about crime and justice. It is striking that six out of the seven variables should be *independently* predictive of perceived lenience. The excluded variable, the estimated proportion of convicted rapists who are sent to

---

3   A recent poll in America found that when respondents were asked to explain increases in crime rates, almost half the sample identified the courts (Maguire and Pastore, 1995). In Canada, over three-quarters of the polled public agreed with the statement that "There is a great deal of crime because sentences are not severe enough" (Brillon, Louis-Guerin and Lamarche, 1984).

4   Predictiveness was taken here from the order in which variables were selected for inclusion in the regression equation according to a forward stepwise procedure.

prison, was quite closely intercorrelated with the equivalent variable for mugging (Pearsons r = +.4); if the latter is excluded from the analysis, the former emerges as a significant predictor.

Table 3.6 illustrates the relationship between misperceptions and attitudes using a different analytic approach. It contrasts the opinions of respondents who were the best- and least-informed about crime and justice. We have defined the best informed as the one in 20 who provided accurate answers to four or more out of seven questions testing knowledge of crime and justice. The least informed were the one in four who were wrong on all seven counts.

Table 3:6 Opinions about sentencers, by level of knowledge about crime and justice

	Least informed (n=2143) %	Best informed (n=376) %	Total sample %
Sentences are:			
Too tough	2	5	3
About right	12	37	19
Too lenient	86	58	79
Judges are:			
In touch	14	29	18
A bit out of touch	34	40	36
Very out of touch	52	31	46
Magistrates are:			
In touch	31	53	37
A bit out of touch	42	36	42
Very out of touch	26	11	21

Note: the seven "knowledge" questions were:
1.   Trends in recorded crime over past two years (correct answer: same or less)
2.   Percentage of recorded incidents that are violent (correct answer: 25%)
3.   Percentage of recorded crimes cleared up (correct answer: 20% to 30%)
4.   Percentage of men with criminal record by the age of 40 (correct answer: 35% to 45%)
5.   Percentage of convicted rapists sent to prison (correct answer: 85% to 100%)
6.   Percentage of convicted muggers sent to prison (correct answer: 60% to 79%)
7.   Percentage of convicted burglars sent to prison (correct answer: 50% to 69%)

Table 3.7 Demographic breakdown of the proportion of the sample making large underestimates of imprisonment rates

	Percentage making large underestimates of imprisonment rate for............		
	Burglary	Mugging	Rape
Educational attainment			
A levels +	52%	59%	42%
Lower	56%	64%	63%
Newspaper preference			
Tabloid	58%	66%	63%
Mail/Express	56%	62%	56%
Local	56%	63%	58%
Broadsheet	49%	58%	41%
None	53%	58%	59%
Social class			
Non-manual	55%	62%	52%
Manual	56%	63%	61%
Sex			
Males	56%	61%	46%
Females	54%	63%	66%
Age			
16–29	47%	62%	53%
30–59	58%	63%	54%
60+	54%	61%	65%
Housing			
Owner	56%	62%	55%
Renter	50%	62%	61%
Household income			
Under £15K	54%	62%	65%
£15K +	56%	62%	49%
Ethnic group			
White	56%	62%	57%
Black	38%	58%	61%
Asian	46%	62%	54%

Who underestimates sentence severity?

The probability that misperceptions about crime and justice are fuelling public dissatisfaction makes it important to know which demographic groups are especially misinformed about sentencing. Table 3.7 shows what groups are most likely to under-estimate sentencing severity. Overall, those who make large underestimates are likely to be poorly educated readers of tabloid newspapers. There are few consistent patterns for age, sex, class, income and race; however, women, those from manual households, older people and the least affluent were more likely than others to underestimate the use of imprisonment for rapists. Whites and owner occupiers were more likely than others to do so in relation to burglars.

To assess which demographic variables best predicted the tendency to underestimate the use of imprisonment, we carried out a stepwise logistic regression using as predictor variables all those shown in Table 3.7. The aim of the analysis was to identify the variables which best predicted 'under-estimators'. We defined this group as all those who made large underestimates (defined in Table 2.2) of the use of imprisonment for all three offence categories. Exactly a third of the sample were under-estimators. Poor educational attainment was the best predictor, followed by sex (being female), reading tabloid newspapers, being over 50 and finally, being an owner occupier. The fact that sex is a predictor reflects the fact that women are more likely than men to underestimate rape sentences; that owner-occupation is a predictor reflects the fact that owners underestimate the severity of sentences for burglary.[5]

---

5 The analysis was carried out using weighted data. Similar findings emerged for the unweighted data-set, except that the order of entry of the last two variables was reversed.

26

Sentencing preferences in specific cases

The implications of the preceding analysis are clear: it would be inappropriate for sentencers to respond to public dissatisfaction by toughening up sentencing policy. At least in part, public dissatisfaction stems from public ignorance of the system. In a sentencing climate in which public misperceptions about crime and sentencing are pervasive, the only safe way of assessing the acceptability of current practice is to elicit people's sentencing preferences for particular categories of crime, and to compare their preferences to practice. Even then, it is clear that the category of crime needs to be specified in some detail. When people are asked general questions, they will answer with the worst case in mind. Previous research has shown that when people respond to a question of this kind, most are thinking of a violent offender with several, related previous convictions (e.g., Doob and Roberts, 1988). This explains, in part at least, the punitive response. The public is not "sentencing" the average offender coming before the courts, but rather of the worst case scenario.

The approach followed in the 1996 BCS was to describe a real case, which went to the Court of Appeal, and to get respondents to select a sentence (or sentences, as multiple choices were permitted). The details of the case were presented on a show-card as follows:

> *A man aged 23 pleaded guilty to the burglary of a cottage belonging to an elderly man whilst he was out during the day. The offender, who had previous convictions for burglary, took a video worth £150 and a television which he left damaged near the scene of the crime.*

The offender had been given a three-year sentence in the Crown Court, which was reduced on appeal to two years. Had such a case appeared before magistrates, it would almost certainly have attracted a custodial sentence, and probably would have attracted the maximum of six months. Crown Court sentences for similar cases might range from six months to two years.

In getting respondents to "sentence" the offender, we varied the method of asking the question. Two-thirds of the sample were first provided with a list of sentencing alternatives,[6] and were then asked to choose one or more punishments. However, the remaining third, selected to constitute half the sample of non-victims, were denied the "menu" of sentencing options. (Victims had to be excluded from the sub-sample, as they had already been given the menu earlier in the interview, when asked about ways of punishing "their" offender.) The hypothesis being tested was that the top-of-the-head reaction of most people is to think first and foremost about imprisonment.

Table 3.8 presents findings for the majority of the sample, excluding the sub-set of non-victims who "sentenced" without a menu of options. It shows that imprisonment was the most favoured option. However, only slightly more than half of respondents favoured imprisonment; a fifth favoured a fine, and around a third favoured community penalties other than a fine. These responses are on balance more lenient than either the Court of Appeal judgement or the Magistrates Association guidelines which suggest that the 'entry point' sentence for a domestic burglary of this sort is a short prison sentence.

It is also noteworthy that in the series of questions asking for estimates of the proportion of convicted adult offenders who *are* and *ought to be* imprisoned, respondents on average said that 80 per cent of burglars should go to prison. By implication, this – very typical – example of burglary fell in the eyes of the public at the less serious end of the spectrum. This underscores how useless for policy it is to provide survey findings pitched at a general level. If the general public overestimates the seriousness of the average burglary, as appears to be the case here, those responsible for sentencing policy can derive little of value from the finding that, on average, people think that 80 per cent of burglars should be locked up.

Table 3:8 Sentencing preferences in Court of Appeal burglary (excluding sub-sample who sentenced without "menu")

Sentencing option	Percentage of respondents choosing %
Imprisonment	54
Suspended sentence	18
Fine	21
Probation	9
Community service	26
Tagging	11
Compensation	44
Discharge	1

Note: columns exceed 100% due to multiple selections by respondents

Respondents who chose sentences using the sentencing menu fell into

---

6   The alternatives were: imprisonment; suspended prison sentence; fine; probation; community service order; electronic tagging; compensation; conditional discharge.

roughly equal groups of non-victims and victims (i.e., those who had reported any victimisation as occurring within 1995). Common sense might suggest that victims would be more punitive than non-victims. In the event, this was not the case: 55 per cent of the victim sample favoured imprisonment, compared with 53 per cent of non-victims. It might be thought that this merely reflects the large number of victims of relatively trivial incidents. However, when victims of burglary (whether attempted or successful) are analysed separately, again a similar proportion (53%) favour imprisonment for the Court of Appeal offender. The view that victims are more punitive than non-victims, then, was not supported by these findings.

As we had expected, the sub-sample who had to choose a sentence without the benefit of a sentencing menu opted more often for prison. Table 3.9 shows the sentencing choices of those who sentenced with and without the menu of options.

It can be seen that just over two-thirds of the "non-menu" sub-sample favoured a term of custody, whereas only half of the other group endorsed imprisonment as a sanction. This is a highly significant difference. Respondents provided with a list of options were more likely to favour imposition of a suspended sentence, probation and community service. Support for compensation was also higher when respondents were aware that it was an option: almost half (44%) of the "menu" group chose compensation, compared with 22 per cent of the "non-menu" group.

Table 3.9 Sentencing preferences as a function of awareness of options

Percentage of respondents choosing sentencing options	Sentencing options provided to respondent	No sentencing options provided
	%	%
Imprisonment	**54**	**67**
Suspended sentence	18	8
Fine	21	19
Probation	9	5
Community service	26	20
Tagging	11	4
Compensation	44	22
Discharge	1	1

Note: columns exceed 100% due to multiple selections by respondents

As for sentence length, the median[7] term of imprisonment favoured by respondents was 12 months. This result will also surprise those who believe that the British public are highly punitive. After all, the case involved a vulnerable victim, loss of property, and most important of all, the offender had several previous convictions for the same offence.[8] It is hard, on the basis of these findings, to argue that the public are consistently more severe than the courts. After all, the Court of Appeal sentenced the offender to two years in prison, while almost half the public favoured a community-based sanction. And, of those members of the public who did choose imprisonment, only a quarter exceeded the Court of Appeal sentence.

Summary

This chapter has shown in unusually stark terms that the public in England and Wales take a jaundiced view of sentencers and sentencing. Judges in particular are regarded as out of touch with the public, and four-fifths of people think that sentences are too lenient. The BCS has demonstrated equally clearly, however, that at least in part, public dissatisfaction is grounded in ignorance of current practice, and in ignorance of current crime trends. Those who are most dissatisfied are most likely to overestimate the growth in crime and the degree to which crime is violent, underestimate the courts' use of imprisonment and underestimate the clear-up rate. Those who are most likely to underestimate the courts' use of imprisonment have lower educational attainment than others, and are more likely to read tabloid newspapers. When people are asked about a specific case, their sentencing prescriptions are, on balance, well in line with current sentencing practice.

---

7   The mean length of imprisonment was higher, but this was an instance in which the average was skewed by some very extreme scores: 1% of the sample chose sentence lengths in excess of 20 years. For this reason, we feel that the median is the most appropriate measure of central tendency.

8   Research has shown that like the courts, members of the public become far more punitive when the offender being sentenced has several related previous convictions (see Roberts, 1997).

4 Strategies for controlling crime

This chapter presents the results of a set of questions designed to explore what role people saw sentencing as having in crime control, what alternatives they envisaged as effective, and the perceived costs and benefits of imprisonment as a crime control strategy. The questions covered the following topics:

- the role of sentencing in causing crime

- the most effective way of preventing crime

- strategies for reducing prison overcrowding

- the impact of imprisonment on offending.

The role of sentencing in causing crime

In the last chapter we discussed the relationship between perceptions of the influence that sentencing has upon the crime rate and evaluations of the judiciary. At this point we explore in greater depth public beliefs about the relationship between sentencing patterns and crime rates. The public in many countries appear to believe that lenient sentencing is a cause of increasing crime rates. This issue was explored in this survey in the following way. Those who stated that they believed the crime rate had increased or decreased over the previous two years were asked: *"You said earlier that you thought that the recorded crime rate had increased/decreased over the past two years. What role would you say that lenient/tough sentencing by the courts has played in this increase/decrease?"* They were provided with four response alternatives: (a) the most important cause; (b) a major cause, but not the most important; (c) only a minor cause; (d) not a cause of this change.

As discussed in Chapter 2, three-quarters of the sample thought that crime had risen over the last two years; they were asked whether *lenient* sentencing had played a part. They saw a clear link. A quarter thought that sentencing patterns were the most important cause, and 48 per cent saw it as a major cause, of rising crime (see Table 4.1). If people believe that lenient sentencing causes crime, then by inference they probably also believe that harsher sentencing would have a preventive effect, resulting in lower crime rates. These results suggest that a majority of the British public appear to subscribe to a perception of sentencing as a crime control mechanism.[1] Sentencing is accorded rather less weight when similar questions are asked in different contexts. For example, ONS's omnibus survey carried a module of questions about drug-crime. In this, only 37 per cent of respondents identified lenient sentencing as a 'main cause' of crime, compared with 65 per cent who opted for drug misuse (Charles, forthcoming).

The four per cent of respondents who thought – accurately – that recorded crime rates were falling were asked whether tough sentencing had played a part in this. Opinion was divided fairly evenly between those who thought that sentencing was unrelated, a minor cause and a major cause.

Table 4.1 Relationship between perceptions of changes in the crime rate and the cause of this change

	Crime in the country as a whole	
	There is more	There is less
Sentencing is:		
Most important cause	26%	6%
A major cause	48%	25%
A minor cause	20%	35%
Not a cause	6%	33%
	100%	100%

---

1   In this respect their perceptions are at odds with reality. There is general agreement among sentencing scholars that changes in sentencing severity will have little impact on the overall crime rate. One reason for this is that such a small percentage of offences are ever prosecuted. In England and Wales, some two per cent of offences result in the imposition of a sentence (Home Office, 1994). Increasing the average sentence, say, from six months to two years will have no appreciable impact on the overall crime rate. Ashworth (1995) concludes that: "It should therefore be clear that, if criminal justice policy expects sentencing to perform a major preventive function, it is looking in the wrong direction" (p. 23).

The most effective way of preventing crime

Two questions addressed public opinion regarding the most effective way of preventing crime. Respondents were first asked which of a series of ways to prevent crime would be effective. This was not a free response question; they were given a list of six strategies and were allowed to choose up to six options. After having identified the crime prevention strategies which in their view would be effective, respondents who had given more than one response were then asked to choose the single strategy which in their opinion would be the most effective. Since the same hierarchy of options emerged from both questions, for ease of presentation, we shall present the results from the latter question only (Table 4.2).

In response to the question about the single most effective strategy, the following hierarchy emerged. *"Increase discipline in the family"* attracted the largest number of respondents, 36 per cent of the sample.[2] This was followed by "reduce levels of unemployment" (25%); "make sentences tougher" (20%); "increase the number of police officers" (9%); "increase discipline in schools" (8%); and finally "increase the use of community-based penalties such as fines and community service" (2%). Thus even though most people believe that lenient sentencing is a major cause of increasing crime rates, the public has a broad, multidimensional view of crime prevention, one which does not place exclusive or even primary emphasis on harsher sentencing. The British public, like their counterparts in North America[3] and Australia, appear to believe that there are several causes of crime, and that this must be reflected in any crime prevention strategy.

Table 4.2 Views about relative effectiveness of crime prevention strategies

Which is the most effective in preventing crime?

1. Increase discipline in the home	36%
2. Reduce levels of unemployment	25%
3. Make sentences tougher	20%
4. Increase the number of police officers	9%
5. Increase discipline in schools	8%
6. Increase use of community-based sentences such as fines, community service	2%
	100%

---

2   The 1997 ONS Omnibus Survey discussed above also found that poor parental discipline was the most frequently identified 'main cause' of crime.

3   When Canadians were given the same list, only 27 per cent chose "making sentences harsher"; (see Roberts and Grossman, 1991).

The criminal justice alternatives (tougher sentencing; more police officers) together attract less than one-third of the responses. Thus although earlier questions have established that lenient sentencing is a concern to the British public, four out of five people see the most effective solution to crime as lying outside the criminal justice system, namely in the home, the schools and the workplace.[4] These trends are worth noting as they contradict the view of the public as being exclusively oriented towards punishment. The British public do want harsher sentences (or at least harsher than they believe them to be), but more punitive sentencing is not seen as the panacea for rising crime.

As with many other issues in this survey, responses to this question were related to perceptions of sentencing severity. Table 4.3 shows that of those who felt sentences were too lenient, only 21 per cent favoured reducing unemployment as the most effective crime prevention strategy. Reducing unemployment was chosen by 49 per cent of those who thought that sentences were too tough and 39 per cent of those who believed that sentences were about right.

Table 4.3 Relationship between perceptions of sentencing trends and choice of most effective crime prevention strategy

	Sentences are too tough	Sentences are about right	Sentences are too lenient
Most effective way of preventing crime is:			
Increase discipline in the family	27%	33%	37%
Increase discipline in schools	5%	8%	8%
Reduce unemployment	49%	39%	21%
Increase number of police	8%	7%	9%
Make sentences tougher	10%	8%	23%
Increase use of community sanctions	2%	4%	2%
Total	100%	100%	100%

---

4   The reactions of the public in North America are comparable. In response to a similar question, less than a third of Canadians regarded criminal justice solutions as the most effective way to prevent crime (Roberts and Grossman, 1991).

Strategies for reducing prison overcrowding

The overcrowded state of British prisons has also been the subject of considerable news media coverage, including widespread publicity surrounding "prison ships". Respondents were told that there is some evidence that the prisons are overcrowded, and were then asked to choose one of three ways of addressing the problem. One solution emerged with far more support from the public than the others. *"Find new ways to punish offenders that are less expensive than prison but tougher than probation"* was chosen by over half the respondents (56%), while the next most popular solution to overcrowding (supported by almost one-quarter of the sample) was to *"release some non-violent offenders from prison earlier than at present with more probation supervision after release".*

The least favoured solution to overcrowding in prisons was the option to *"build more prisons and pay for them by raising taxes or cutting spending in other areas".* This was endorsed by only 18 per cent of the respondents. Clearly then, additional prison construction, however it is financed, is an option that is supported by few members of the public. Here too there are parallels with responses to this question in other countries, where support for intermediate sanctions (those lying between imprisonment and probation) exceeds support for prison construction by a considerable margin (c.f. Roberts, 1992; Roberts and Stalans, 1997).

If people's attention had not been drawn to the cost of prison building, it is probable that support for this strategy would have been stronger. It strikes us as more sensible when canvassing opinion not to offer respondents a "free lunch"; unless their attention is drawn to opportunity costs, the public generally want more and better public services of every sort.

Impact of imprisonment on offending

The prison is central to a layperson's conceptions of punishment. When most people think about sentencing, they think about lengths of imprisonment. It is important therefore to know about attitudes towards, and knowledge of, prison life. To explore this issue, respondents were asked to agree or disagree with three statements. The first dealt with employment training. Almost three-quarters (71%) of respondents agreed with the statement that *"in prison offenders receive training for jobs".* Only 16 per cent disagreed with the statement. (Twelve per cent neither agreed nor disagreed with the statement.) Thus most of the public are aware of this aspect of prison life. Less than half the sample (46%) agreed with the following statement: *"In prison, offenders are helped to become law-abiding citizens."* This is confirmation of a widespread disenchantment with the effectiveness of prisons in terms of promoting law-abiding behaviour. Over one-third (36%) disagreed with the statement, while 17 per cent neither agreed nor disagreed.

If prisons do not encourage law-abiding behaviour, do they at least punish those serving time? The public appear to believe so. Just over one-half of the sample agreed that *"being put in prison punishes offenders"*. Fewer than one-third disagreed with the statement and 20 per cent neither agreed nor disagreed. An interesting relationship emerged when responses to this question were cross-tabulated with responses to the question about sentence severity. Respondents who believed that sentences were too lenient were also less likely to subscribe to the view that prison punishes offenders, as Table 4.4 shows.

Table 4.4 Relationship between perceptions of sentencing and whether prison serves as a punishment

| | Sentences are: | |
	Too lenient	About right
Prison punishes	48%	65%
No opinion	20%	18%
Prison does not punish	32%	17%
	100%	100%

This relationship suggests that one reason so many people think sentences should be harsher is that they believe that imprisonment is not that aversive an experience for inmates.

One criticism of prisons that has been around for many generations is that they may in fact promote criminal behaviour by encouraging the transmission of ways in which to offend. The public would appear to subscribe strongly to this view. More than four out of five respondents (82%) agreed with the statement that *"In prison, offenders learn new ways to commit crime"*. Only six per cent of the sample disagreed with the statement. (A further 11% neither agreed nor disagreed.)

Although many people have strong views about prison life, and how a prison should be run, few people have any direct experience with custodial settings. Respondents were asked *"Have you ever been inside a prison, as a visitor, or for any other reason?"*. Four out of five respondents stated that they had never been in a prison in any capacity. We carried out analysis to see if direct experience with prison bore any relation to attitudes towards prison.

Surprisingly, the only significant difference which we found was that those with direct experience were more likely to agree with the statement that prisons help inmates to become law-abiding citizens: 44 per cent, compared to only 35% of respondents without experience of prison.

Summary

Findings presented in this chapter show that most people recognise that many different factors underlie current levels of crime. They generally believe that sentencing is an important determinant. However, they tend to see changes in parenting and in unemployment levels as more promising ways of reducing crime. Their attitudes towards greater use of imprisonment is at least ambivalent, with a widespread belief in the negative potential of imprisonment in stimulating further crime, and a greater preference expressed for tougher community penalties than for building new prisons.

5 The views of victims

In this section, we take a closer look at the responses of victims of crime. Victims have been asked the same question in every BCS sweep since 1984, asking what punishment "their" offender should receive. The format of the question has remained essentially unchanged, allowing analysis of trends over the 12-year period. We have focussed here on residential burglary involving losses (i.e., excluding all forms of unsuccessful burglary) and theft of cars, partly because these are relatively homogeneous categories of crime and partly because almost all incidents are reported to the police.[1] Figure 5.1 presents the results.

Figure 5.1 shows an increase between 1984 and 1996 from 33 per cent to 48 per cent in the proportion of burglary victims who want their offender imprisoned. Unlike the findings presented above, these estimates are based on small numbers (especially in earlier sweeps) and are subject to significant sampling error.[2] Nonetheless, it seems clear that victims of burglary have become more punitive over the 12 years since 1984. Victims of car theft show a similar pattern, with the proportion favouring imprisonment rising from 17 per cent in 1984 to 44 per cent in 1996. It should be remembered that concern about joyriders was of particular public and political concern in 1991 and 1992[3] – though the difference between the 1992 and 1996 figures is not statistically significant.

---

1   Ninety-two per cent of burglaries with loss and 99 per cent of car thefts (including unauthorised taking) were reported in the 1992 BCS. If unreported crimes are excluded from Figure 3.3, the proportion of burglary victims favouring imprisonment increases three percentage points to 44 per cent; there is no change for victims of car theft.

2   Assuming minimal design effects, the estimate of 33 per cent of burglary victims favouring imprisonment in 1984 may have a true value anywhere between 27 per cent and 39 per cent, and the corresponding figure of 49 per cent for 1996 may have a true value anywhere between 45 per cent and 53 per cent (p<.05).

3   A series of serious road accidents involving stolen cars coupled with media accounts of joyriding in places such as the Blackbird Lees Estate near Oxford led to the Aggravated Vehicle Taking Act, 1992.

Figure 5.1 Victims' preferred sentence

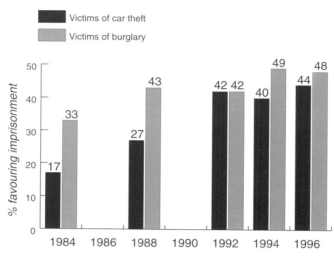

Note: No BCS in 1986 and 1990.

It might be argued that the increasing enthusiasm for imprisoning burglars reflects not a growing punitiveness but an increase in the average seriousness of cases. The BCS provides only partial support for this. In each sweep, victims were asked to assign a score between 0 and 20 reflecting their perceptions of the seriousness of their crime. The average score for burglary increased from 8.0 in 1984 to 9.7 in 1992, then falling back to 9.2 in 1996. Interpretation of such a scale is complex. How victims manage to locate their crime on this scale is a mysterious process. The scores may generally reflect the objective level of harm done by the offender or the seriousness with which victims felt they should be dealt. If the former, then the increase in victims' desire for imprisonment over the period 1984–1992 might reflect an increase in the average seriousness of cases, but the increase from 1992–1996 does not.

The 1992 BCS allows comparison between victims' responses to the question about their "own" offender and that about offenders in analogous vignettes. Table 5.1 makes this comparison for victims of burglary and of car theft. Numbers are even smaller – and imprecision even greater – than for Figure 5.1, because only half of the sample completed that section of the questionnaire involving the vignettes. Sentence preferences for "own" offender are also slightly different from those in Figure 5.1, for the same reason. The table shows that victims were more likely to advocate imprisonment for "their" offender than for the one in the vignette – somewhat so in relation to burglary, markedly so for car theft. The most likely reason for this is that on average, victims suffered more serious crimes than those in the vignettes.[4] It is also possible – but not empirically testable in the 1992 BCS – that people judge that crimes in which they have been the victim deserve heavier punishment than similar crimes committed against others.

Table 5:1 Victims' preferred sentences for 'their' offender and analogous offender in vignette

	Crime			
	Burglary with loss		Car theft	
	Own burglary	Vignette	Own car theft	Vignette
Sentence	%	%	%	%
Prison	44	36	45	24
Fine	7	12	15	23
Community service	20	13	11	6
Probation, susp. sent	7	11	7	12
Compensation	6	13	16	15
Discharge or caution	6	9	4	18
Other/DK/depends	10	7	2	3
	–	–	–	–
	100	100	100	100

Notes: British Crime Survey, 1992. Weighted data. All burglaries involve entry to home and theft of property. Car thefts include incidents which would be recorded by the police as unauthorised taking.

The 1992 BCS can provide some tentative clues as to whether the experience of victimisation fuels punitive attitudes towards offenders in general, as responses to the vignettes can be broken down according to respondents' status as victims of crime. Thus for example, 36 per cent of the 175 burglary victims who completed the sentencing questionnaire advocated imprisonment for the burglar in the vignette, compared with 30 per cent of the overall sample. Corresponding figures for car theft are 24 per cent of victims, and 20 per cent of the overall sample. These figures may seem suggestive of a causal link between victimisation and punitive attitudes, but the differences do not approach statistical significance. This finding is consistent with the results from the 1996 survey which we

---

4   Of those BCS respondents who were victims of burglary involving loss in 1991, 55% suffered losses of at least £500, and a further 14% had losses between £250 and £500. The burglary vignette specified the loss of a video-recorder - whose average value in 1992 was probably lower than this. Similarly, the vignette for car theft specified that the car was recovered undamaged; in over two thirds of BCS car thefts in 1991, the vehicle suffered at least £100 of damage or was never recovered.

summarised in an earlier section of this report. Provisionally, and in line with other work (Brillon, 1988; Hough and Moxon, 1985; van Dijk and Steinmetz, 1988) the conclusion must be that experience as victim of crime does not fuel punitiveness in any marked way.

Summary

Over time, there has been a marked increase in victims' preference for tough sentencing, at least in relation to two types of crime, burglary and car theft. There is no evidence to suggest that this trend is a function simply of increasing severity of the average crime of this sort. Consistent with findings reported in Chapter 2, there is no evidence that the experience of victimisation fuels a desire for tougher penalties.

6 Conclusions

Several themes emerge from this, the most extensive analysis to date of British attitudes toward sentencing and related criminal justice issues. First, the general perception of leniency by the courts is widespread, and is clearly related to evaluations of the judiciary, and to a lesser extent, magistrates. While the perception persists that sentences are too lenient, criticism of judges and magistrates will continue. Judges received the most negative evaluations of all criminal justice professionals in this survey. The lesson would appear clear: clarifying public misperception about sentencing trends in this country will promote public confidence in judges and magistrates. And, since the judiciary occupy such a critical place in the criminal justice system, increasing confidence in the courts will promote confidence in the administration of justice. Since the perception of leniency has been around for two decades now, it constitutes a priority in terms of public education.

However, the public also need more accurate information about issues related to sentencing. As we have seen from the BCS results reported here, part of the public misperception about sentencing involves a link between sentencing patterns and crime rates. In the light of this connection, it is important to educate the public about trends in crime and the proportion of crime that involves violence. Otherwise, people will continue to believe that crime rates are increasing inexorably (particularly rates of violent crime), and they will be inclined to attribute this increase to lenient sentencing. In this way, the cycle of disappointment with sentencing and criticism of the judiciary can only continue.

It would be wrong to characterise the British public as being highly punitive, or as being consistently more punitive than judges. The public adhere to what may be termed a multi-track approach to the punishment of offenders. First, the public do not look exclusively to the courts to prevent crime. Crime prevention is seen as a problem for society at large; it is not regarded primarily as a criminal justice issue. Politicians may advocate tougher sentencing in order to "do something about the crime problem", but many members of the public believe that reducing the crime rate is more a question of changing the family and school environment, and increasing the number of people with jobs. This is not to say that the public see no role for sentencing in preventing crime; responses to the BCS indicate that lenient sentencing is seen as being a cause of crime, but tougher sentencers are not seen as the only or even the primary remedy.

While the public respond to polls by endorsing the view that sentences are too lenient, this result must be seen in light of the findings reported in this paper and elsewhere. When asked about sentencing in general, the public think of the worst kinds of offenders (recidivists) and the most serious crimes of violence, who represent a small minority of the total offender population. When presented with a complete description of an actual case, the public tend to be less punitive. As well, when given adequate information about the range of legal punishments available, the public are less likely to endorse the use of imprisonment. Another way of stating this is to say that when members of the public have a level of information comparable to that which is available to a judge in a court, the public respond in a way that is fairly consistent with judicial practice. This result has emerged from a wealth of research in several countries, and now emerges from the 1992 and 1996 British Crime Surveys.[1]

It is worth reiterating the point that the British public are not alone in holding a number of misperceptions about crime and justice. Throughout this report we have noted parallels with public reactions to sentencing in several other western nations. The British public are no less informed, or no more critical than the public in these other countries.

On the basis of the International Crime Victimisation Survey (Mayhew and van Dijk, 1997), the proportion of the public favouring tougher penalties has risen rather than fallen over the period since 1992 when the use of imprisonment has been growing rapidly. Given the findings presented in Chapter 1, it is more plausible that perceptions of leniency are independent of actual sentencing practices. People assume that sentences are lenient, whatever the reality, the same way that they probably assume prices are rising, regardless of the actual rate of inflation. Increasing the use of imprisonment for some offence – say burglary – from 50 per cent to 90 per cent would not assuage public concern over sentencing trends, since the public would remain unaware of the shift in sentencing patterns. The reason for this degree of misinformation of course is that people do not receive information about sentencing practices in the news media, but rather a steady stream of stories about sentencing malpractice, cases in which a judge imposes what appears to be a very lenient sentence for a serious crime of violence.

---

1   It is also consistent with findings derived from earlier sweeps of the BCS.

The news media make no attempt to explain the judicial reasoning underlying the decision, or to place the sentence imposed in some statistical context. In order to reconcile the public and the courts, a rational approach must involve informing people about the nature of sentencing practices.

The most challenging demands are in identifying effective ways of interrupting the processes which feed public cynicism. To date very limited use has been made of the communication techniques of the late twentieth century in letting the public know about current sentencing practice. All commercial operations of any significance market themselves, and most public institutions now do so. The court system may not be entirely unique in continuing with eighteenth century strategies of pomp and ritual to sustain its authority. However, a successful strategy for tackling public misperceptions will almost certainly have to resort to more modern techniques. It will have to identify key audiences, such as opinion formers, victims, potential offenders and people at risk of offending, and convey in media appropriate to each audience an accurate portrayal of current sentencing practice.

Appendix A: Organisation and design of the British Crime Survey

The British Crime Survey (BCS) has been carried out six times, in 1982, 1984, 1987, 1992, 1994 and 1996. This appendix summarises the design of the 1996 sweep. Previous sweeps differed only in minor detail. The 1996 British Crime Survey was carried out in early 1996 by Social and Community Planning Research (SCPR)[1]. Design of the survey was shared between staff of the Home Office Research and Planning Unit and SCPR. Full details of the survey's methodology are to be found in SCPR's technical report (Hales and Stratford, 1997), and are summarised in Mirrlees-Black et al. (1996).

Sampling

The 1996 BCS comprised a 'core' sample and various supplementary samples, none of which only are relevant to this analysis. (As in the three previous sweeps, the 1996 survey carried an additional 'booster' sample of black and Asian respondents. However, the questions on attitudes to punishment were not asked of this subsample.) The core sample was designed to give, after appropriate weighting, a representative cross-section both of private households in England and Wales and of individuals aged 16 and over in such households. As in 1992 and 1994, but not in earlier sweeps, the Postcode Address File (PAF) was used in 1996 as the sampling frame as it represents the fullest register of household addresses. (The PAF is a listing of all postal delivery points in the country, almost all households having one delivery point, or letter box.) As in previous years, inner city areas were oversampled by a factor of about two. The 1996 definition of inner cities approximates to that used in the three previous sweeps, classifying postcode sectors on the basis of population density, level of owner-occupied tenure and proportion of households with heads of households in 'professional' jobs.

---

[1]   SCPR did the fieldwork in the first survey; NOP Market Research in the second, and a consortium of both companies in the third; a consortium of SCPR and BMRB did the fourth; and OPCS did the fifth.

The sample design required selection of 800 postcode sectors as primary sampling units (PSUs). These were selected from a stratified list of sectors, with stratifying factors being (i) inner city or not, (ii) standard region and (iii) social class of household head. Once postcode sectors had been selected, 27 addresses were randomly selected from each (30 in inner cities). Then, where there were two or more dwelling units at an address (2% of the total), interviewers randomly selected one. Finally, in dwelling units with two or more person aged 16+, interviewers selected one, using a randomising procedure.

Fieldwork

The 1996 core sample covered a nationally representative sample of 16,348 households in England and Wales. The response rate was 82.5% for the core, higher than in the previous four years by five percentage points. One adult (defined as 16 or older) in each household was interviewed. Computer assisted personal interviewing (CAPI) procedures were used.

Structure of the questionnaire

These were several parts to the questionnaire: the Main Questionnaire; Victim Forms (a maximum of six per respondent, with the fourth, fifth and sixth forms being truncated versions); one of two possible Follow-up Questionnaires, a further set of questions on household fires, the Demographic Questionnaire and two Self-completion Questionnaires (which covered questions about drugs for those aged 16-59 and questions about experience of domestic violence for women aged 16-59). Of the two versions of the Follow-up Questionnaire, Follow Up A focused on contact with the police, neighbourhood watch, home security and fear of crime; and Follow Up B covered attitudes to punishment. The rationale for introducing different follow-up questionnaires was that the largely attitudinal questions asked at this stage of the interview did not require the same precision as those in other parts; it made sense, therefore, to split the sample into two, extending topic coverage at little cost in terms of precision. The selected adult respondent in each household completed the Main, Demographic and one or other version of the Follow-up Questionnaires. Victim Forms were completed only by those who said they had experienced a crime since the beginning of 1993.

Weighting

Data from the survey were weighted in a number of ways at the data processing stage. Weighting served two main purposes: to correct imbalances introduced in sampling; and to correct imbalances created by the design of the interview. Weights were applied to correct for:

- the over-representation of inner city residents

- cases where more than one household was covered by an entry on the PAF file

- the fact that individuals living in larger households were under-represented (as the chance of an adult being selected for interview was inversely related to the number of adults in that household).

Sampling error and design effects

The sampling design, particularly the stratification and degree of clustering of addresses, has an effect on the statistical reliability of the results. A design factor quantifies this effect on estimates, and is a measure of the expected variability of estimates from repeated samples of the sample design, relative to a simple random sample. Some examples of design effects for personal crime rates (using the same weighting procedure as in this report) are to be found in Hales and Stratford (1997). Design factors for the core sample typically ranged from unity to 1.4.

Appendix B: Extract from the 1996 British Crime Survey questionnaire

This is a transcript of the questions presented on the computer screen to the interviewer when running the 1998 BCS CAPI programme. It may, therefore, differ in some respects from the CAPI interview.

E.1   Attitudes to sentencing

CrimUK   [ASK ALL] I would like to ask whether you think that the recorded crime rate for the country as a whole has changed over the past two years. Would you say there is more crime, less crime or about the same amount (since two years ago)? PROBE. Is that a lot or a little more/less?

        1.   A lot more crime
        2.   A little more crime
        3.   About the same
        4.   A little less crime
        5   A lot less crime

Nvio   [ASK ALL] The next few questions are about your perceptions of the level of crime. If you don't know an answer, please give us your best guess. We are equally interested in what you think the answers might be. For several of these questions we will be asking you to give an answer out of 100, for example out of every 100 crimes how many are a particular type of crime.

Of every 100 crimes recorded by the police, roughly what number do you think involve violence or the threat of violence? PROMPT if you don't know, please just guess.

0 ... 100

Nmurd   [ASK ALL] How many recorded murders do you think there were in England and Wales last year? PROMPT if you don't know, please just guess.

0 ...99997

ClearUp   [ASK ALL] Crimes are recorded as cleared up by the police when the offender is prosecuted or otherwise admits guilt. Out of every 100 crimes reported to the police, what number do you think are 'cleared up'? PROMPT if you don't know, please just guess.

0 100

M40Rec   [ASK ALL] When someone is convicted of a crime, they will have a criminal record. By the time men reach the age of 40, how many out of 100 do you suppose have a criminal record?

0 ...100

SentSev   [ASK ALL] The next few questions are about sentencing by the courts, that is both the Crown Court and magistrates courts. In general, would you say that sentences handed down by the courts are too tough, about right, or too lenient? PROBE Is that a little too tough/lenient or much too tough/lenient?

1.   Much too tough
2.   A little too tough
3.   About right
4.   A little too lenient
5.   Much too lenient

SentCrim   [ASK ALL] CARD B1 You said earlier that you thought that the recorded crime rate had increased/decreased over the past two years. What role would you say that lenient/tough (Sentsev) sentencing by the courts has played in this increase/decrease? Would you say that sentencing has been......

1.   ...the most important cause
2.   ...a major cause, but not the most important one
3.   ...only a minor cause
4.   ...or not a cause of this change

NPrisCh   [ASK ALL] Over the past two years do you think the proportion of offenders sent to prison has increased, stayed the same or decreased?

    1.   Increased
    2.   Stayed the same
    3.   Decreased

TypSent   [ASK ALL] CARD B2 This card shows a description of an actual criminal case. READ OUT IF NECESSARY: A man aged 23 pleaded guilty to the burglary of a cottage belonging to an elderly man whilst he was out during the day. The offender, who had previous convictions for burglary, took a video worth £150 and a television, which he left damaged near the scene of the crime. ALLOW RESPONDENT TIME TO READ PROPERLY THEN ASK:

TypeSentA [ASK IF Digit (SERIAL NUMBER) = 1 OR 5 OR 9] What type, or types, of sentence do you think the offender should receive?

    1.   Imprisonment
    2.   Suspended prison sentence
    3.   Fine
    4.   Probation
    5.   Community service order
    6.   Electronic tagging
    7.   Have to pay compensation
    8.   Conditional discharge
    9.   Other

TypeSntAO [ASK IF TypeSentA = Other] INTERVIEWER RECORD OTHER

SentType The courts can impose a number of different types of sentences upon people convicted of criminal offences. One of these is immediate imprisonment. Which other types can you think of? PROBE. RECORD EACH MENTIONED IN ORDER (UP TO 8 MENTIONS). CODE ALL THAT APPLY

    1.   Suspended prison sentence
    2.   Fine
    3.   Probation
    4.   Community service order
    5.   Electronic tagging
    6.   Have to pay compensation
    7.   Conditional discharge
    8.   Other

SentTypO   [ASK IF SentType = Other]. INTERVIEWER RECORD OTHER.

TypSentB   [ASK IF Digit (SERIAL NUMBER) = 3 OR 7]. CARD B3. ALLOW
           RESPONDENT TIME TO READ PROPERLY, THEN ASK: There are a
           number of possible sentences which could be imposed in this case. What
           type, or types, of sentence do you think the offender should receive?

           1.   Imprisonment
           2.   Suspended prison sentence
           3.   Fine
           4.   Probation
           5.   Community service order
           6.   Electronic tagging
           7.   Have to pay compensation
           8.   Conditional discharge
           9.   Other

TypSntBO   [ASK IF TypSentB = Other]. INTERVIEWER RECORD OTHER

PrSent   [ASK IF TypeSentA OR TypeSentB = Imprisonment]. How long do you
           think the prison sentence should be?

           1.   In years only
           2.   In months only
           3.   In years and months

PrSentY   [ASK IF PrSent = Year only OR Years and months]. CODE NUMBER OF
           YEARS

           0..30

PrSentM   [ASK IF PrSent = Months only OR Years and months]. CODE NUMBER OF
           MONTHS

           0..30

NRapePr1   [ASK ALL] Now I would like to ask you about the kinds of sentences that
           are imposed for rape, mugging and house burglary. First of all, out of
           every 100 men aged 21 or over who are convicted of rape, how many do
           you think are sent to prison?

           0...100

NRapePr2 And how many do you think should be sent to prison?

0..100

NmuggPr1 [ASK ALL] Now turning to mugging which is theft in the street by means of force or the threat of force, out of every 100 adults aged 21 or over who are convicted of mugging, how many do you think are sent to prison?

0...100

NmuggPr2 And how many do you think should be sent to prison?

0...100

NrBurgPr1 [ASK ALL] Now turning to house burglary out of every 100 adults aged 21 or over who are convicted of house burglary, how many do you think are sent to prison?

0...100

NBurgPr2 And how many do you think should be sent to prison?

0...100

JudTouch [ASK ALL] I would now like to ask for your opinions of judges and magistrates who decide what sentences to give. Firstly, Judges. Do you think that judges are generally in touch or out of touch with what ordinary people think? IF OUT OF TOUCH: Is that a bit out of touch or very out of touch?

1.   In touch
2.   A bit out of touch
3.   Very out of touch

MagTouch [ASK ALL] Do you think that magistrates are generally in touch or out of touch with what ordinary people think? IF OUT OF TOUCH: Is that a bit out of touch or very out of touch?

1.   In touch
2.   A bit out of touch
3.   Very out of touch

InPris   [ASK ALL] Now I would like to ask you some questions about prisons. Have you ever been inside a prison, as a visitor or for any other reason?

1.   Yes
2.   No

Serv1Y   If someone is sentenced to serve 12 months, how long, on average, do you think they will actually spend in prison? PROMPT if you don't know, please just guess. ENTER NUMBER OF MONTHS:

0..

PrSkill   [ASK ALL]. CARD B4 I am going to read out some statements about prison. For each one please choose a phrase from the card to say how much you agree or disagree with it. READ OUT...

In prison, offenders receive training for jobs?

1.   Agree strongly
2.   Agree
3.   Neither agree nor disagree
4.   Disagree
5.   Disagree strongly

PrLawAb   CARD B4. In prison, offenders are helped to become law-abiding citizens?

1.   Agree strongly
2.   Agree
3.   Neither agree nor disagree
4.   Disagree
5.   Disagree strongly

PrPun   CARD B4. Being put in prison punishes offenders?

1.   Agree strongly
2.   Agree
3.   Neither agree nor disagree
4.   Disagree
5.   Disagree strongly

PrCrim   CARD B4. In prison, offenders learn new ways to commit crime?

      1.   Agree strongly
      2.   Agree
      3.   Neither agree nor disagree
      4.   Disagree
      5.   Disagree strongly

OverCrow   [ASK ALL]. CARD B5. There is some evidence that the prisons in this country are overcrowded. Looking at this card which one of these do you think would be the best way of reducing overcrowding?

      1.   Find new ways to punish offenders that are less expensive than prison but tougher than probation

      2.   Release some non-violent offenders from prison earlier than at present with more probation supervision after release

      3.   Build more prisons and pay for them by raising taxes or cutting spending in other areas

PrevCr1   [ASK ALL]. CARD B6. Here is some possible ways of helping to prevent crime in Britain. Which of these ways would in your view be effective in preventing crime? (Enter at most six cases).

      1.   Increase discipline in the family
      2.   Increase discipline in schools
      3.   Reduce levels of unemployment
      4.   Increase the number of police officers
      5.   Make sentences tougher
      6.   Increase the use of community based penalties such a fines and community service

PrevCr2   [ASK IF MORE THAN ONE ANSWER AT PREVCR1]. SHOW CARD B6 . And which one way would in your view be most effective in preventing crime? (Enter code). (SCREEN TO SHOW ONLY THOSE CODES RECORDED AT PREVCR1)

      1.   Increase discipline in the family
      2.   Increase discipline in schools
      3.   Reduce levels of unemployment
      4.   Increase the number of police officers
      5.   Make sentences tougher
      6.   Increase the use of community based penalties such a fines and community service

JobPol   [ASK ALL]. CARD B7 . This card lists some different groups of people who collectively form the criminal justice system. We would like to know how good a job you think each off these groups of people are doing.

How good the Police are doing? Would that be an excellent, good, fair, poor or very poor job? (Enter code) PROB

1.   Excellent
2.   Good
3.   Fair
4.   Poor
5.   Very poor

JobCPS   How good the Crown Prosecution Service, that is the body responsible for making prosecutions, is doing? Would that be an excellent, good, fair, poor or very poor job? (Enter code)

1.   Excellent
2.   Good
3.   Fair
4.   Poor
5.   Very poor

JobJud   How good judges are doing? Would that be an excellent, good, fair, poor or very poor job? (Enter code)

1.   Excellent
2.   Good
3.   Fair
4.   Poor
5.   Very poor

JobMag   How good magistrates are doing? Would that be an excellent, good, fair, poor or very poor job? (Enter code)

1.   Excellent
2.   Good
3.   Fair
4.   Poor
5.   Very poor

JobPri   How good the prison services are doing? Would that be an excellent, good, fair, poor or very poor job? (Enter code

     1.   Excellent
     2.   Good
     3.   Fair
     4.   Poor
     5.   Very poor

JobProb   How good the probation services are doing? Would that be an excellent, good, fair, poor or very poor job? (Enter code)

     1.   Excellent
     2.   Good
     3.   Fair
     4.   Poor
     5.   Very poor

MediaCov   ALL] CARD B9. Now I would like you to think about coverage of crime in the media, that is television, radio, newspapers and magazines. How good a job you think the media does in providing you with accurate and balanced information about crime? Would that be an excellent, good, fair, poor or very poor job? (Enter code)

     1.   Excellent
     2.   Good
     3.   Fair
     4.   Poor
     5.   Very poor

Newspap   [ASK ALL] CARD B9. Which one of the following daily newspapers do you read most often?(Enter code)

     1.   Daily Express
     2.   Daily Mail
     3.   Daily Mirror
     4.   Daily Star
     5.   Daily Telegraph
     6.   Financial Times
     7.   The Guardian
     8.   The Independent
     9.   The Sun
     10.   The Times
     11.   Local daily newspaper
     12.   Other daily newspaper
     13.   None

NewsPapO   [ASK IF NewsPap = Other] INTERVIEWER RECORD OTHER

References

Ashworth, A. (1995) *Sentencing and Criminal Justice.* Second Edition. London: Butterworths.

Ashworth, A. and Hough, M. (1996) *'Sentencing and the Climate of Opinion'.* Criminal Law Review, 776–787.

Barclay, G . (ed.) (1995) *Information on the Criminal Justice System in England and Wales.* London: Home Office, Research and Statistics Department.

Brillon, Y. (1988) *'Punitiveness, status and ideology in three Canadian provinces',* in N. Walker and M. Hough (eds.) Public Attitudes to Sentencing: Surveys from Five Countries. Aldershot: Gower.

Brillon, Y., Louis-Guerin, C., and Lamarche, M.-C. (1984) *Attitudes of the Canadian Public Toward Crime Policies.* Ottawa: Ministry of the Solicitor General.

Canadian Sentencing Commission. (1987) *Sentencing Reform: A Canadian Approach.* Ottawa: Supply and Services Canada.

Charles, N. (forthcoming) *Public perceptions of drug related crime in 1997.* Home Office Research and Statistics Directorate Research Findings. London: Home Office.

Diamond, S. and Stalans, L. (1989) *'The Myth of Judicial Leniency in Sentencing.'* Behavioral Sciences and the Law, 7: 73–89.

Doble, J. (1996) *Crime and Corrections: The Views of the people of Vermont.* Report available from the authors.

Doob, A. and Roberts, J.V. (1982) *Crime: Some Views of the Canadian Public.* Ottawa: Department of Justice Canada.

Doob, A. and Roberts, J.V. (1988) *'Public punitiveness and public knowledge of the facts: some Canadian surveys.'* In (eds.) N. Walker and Hough, M. Public Attitudes to Sentencing. Surveys from Five Countries. Aldershot: Gower.

English, K., Crouch, J. and Pullen, S. (1989) *Attitudes toward crime: A survey of Colorado Citizens and Criminal Justice Officials*. Denver: Colorado Department of Public Safety.

Flanagan, T. and Longmire, D. (eds.) (1996) *Americans View Crime and Justice*. A National Public Opinion Survey. Thousand Oaks: Sage.

Gibbons, D., Jones, J. and Garabedian, P. (1972) *'Gauging Public Opinion about the Crime Problem.'* Crime and Delinquency, 18: 134-146.

Home Office. (1995) *Criminal Statistics for England and Wales. Supplementary Tables. Volume 2*. London: Her Majesty's Stationery Office.

Hough, M. (1996) *People Talking About Punishment*. The Howard Journal, 35: 191-214.

Hough, M. and Mayhew, P. (1985) *Taking Account of Crime: Key Findings from the Second British Crime Survey*. Home Office Research Study No. 85. London: Her Majesty's Stationery Office.

Hough, M. and Moxon, D. (1985) *'Dealing with Offenders: popular opinion and the Views of Victims.'* The Howard Journal, 24: 160-175.

Huang, W. and Vaughn, M. (1996) *'Support and Confidence: Public Attitudes Toward the Police.'* In: T. Flanagan and D. Longmire (eds.) Americans View Crime and Justice. A National Public Opinion Survey. Thousand Oaks: Sage.

Indermaur, D. (1987) *'Public Perception of Sentencing in Perth, Western Australia.'* Australian and New Zealand Journal of Criminology, 20: 163-183.

Indermaur, D. (1990) *Perceptions of Crime Seriousness and Sentencing: A comparison of court practice and the perceptions of a sample of the public and judges*. Canberra: Criminology Research Council of Australia.

Jowell, R., Curtice, J., Brook, L. and Ahrend, D. (1994) *British Social Attitudes:* 11th Report. Aldershot: Dartmouth.

Lord Bingham (1997) *The Sentence of the Court. Police Foundation Lecture*, July 1997. London: Police Foundation.

Maguire, K. and Pastore, A. (eds.) (1995) *Sourcebook of Criminal Justice Statistics*. U.S. Department of Justice, Bureau of Justice Statistics.

Mayhew, P. and van Dijk. J.J.M. (1997). *Criminal Victimisation in Eleven Industrialised Countries.* The Hague: Research and Documentation Centre.

Mitchell, B. (forthcoming) *'Attitudes to homicide'* British Journal of Criminology.

Mirrlees-Black, C., Mayhew, P. and Percy, A. (1996) *The British Crime Survey.* Home Office Statistical Bulletin, Issue 19/96.

MVA. (1997). *The 1996 Scottish Crime Survey: first results. Crime and Criminal Justice Research Findings No. 16.* Edinburgh: Scottish Office Central Research Unit.

Povey, D., Prime, J. and Taylor, P. (1997) *Notifiable Offences. England and Wales, 1996.* Home Office Statistical Bulletin, Issue 3, March 1997.

Roberts, J.V. (1992) *'Public Opinion, Crime and Criminal Justice.'* In *(ed.)* M. Tonry, *Crime and Justice.* A Review of Research. Volume 16. Chicago: University of Chicago Press.

Roberts, J.V. (1997) *'The Role of Criminal Record in the Sentencing Process.'* In: M. Tonry (ed.) *Crime and Justice.* A Review of Research. Chicago: University of Chicago Press.

Roberts, J.V. and Grossman, M. (1991) *'Crime Prevention and Public Opinion.'* Canadian Journal of Criminology, 32: 75-90.

Roberts, J.V. and Stalans, L. (1997) *Public Opinion, Crime and Criminal Justice.* Colorado: Westview Press.

van Dijk, J. and Steinmetz, C. (1988) *'Pragmatism, ideology and crime control: three Dutch surveys.'* In: Walker, N. and Hough, M. (eds.) Public Attitudes to Sentencing: Surveys from Five Countries. Aldershot: Gower.

Walker, J., Collins, M. and Wilson, P. (1988) *'How the Public Sees Sentencing: An Australian Survey.'* In: N. Walker and M. Hough (eds.) Public Attitudes to Sentencing: Surveys from Five Countries. Aldershot: Gower.

Walker, N. and Hough, M. (1988) (eds.) *Public Attitudes To Sentencing. Surveys from Five Countries.* Aldershot: Gower.

Williams, K., Gibbs, J. and Erickson, M. (1980) *'Public Knowledge of Statutory Penalties: The extent and basis of accurate perception.'* Pacific Sociological Review, 23: 105-128.

Zander, M. and Henderson, P. (1993) *Crown Court Study. Royal Commission on Criminal Justice. Study No. 19.* London: Her Majesty's Stationery Office.

Publications

List of research publications

A list of research reports for the last three years is provided below. A **full** list of publications is available on request from the Research and Statistics Directorate Information and Publications Group.

Home Office Research Studies (HORS)

151. **Drug misuse declared: results of the 1994 British Crime Survey.** Malcom Ramsay and Andrew Percy. 1996.

152. **An Evaluation of the Introduction and Operation of the Youth Court.** David O'Mahony and Kevin Haines. 1996.

153. **Fitting supervision to offenders: assessment and allocation decisions in the Probation Service.** 1996.

155. **PACE: a review of the literature. The first ten years.** David Brown. 1997.

156. **Automatic Conditional Release: the first two years.** Mike Maguire, Brigitte Perroud and Peter Raynor. 1996.

157. **Testing obscenity: an international comparison of laws and controls relating to obscene material.** Sharon Grace. 1996.

158. **Enforcing community sentences: supervisors' perspectives on ensuring compliance and dealing with breach.** Tom Ellis, Carol Hedderman and Ed Mortimer. 1996.

160. **Implementing crime prevention schemes in a multi-agency setting: aspects of process in the Safer Cities programme.** Mike Sutton. 1996.

161. **Reducing criminality among young people: a sample of relevant programmes in the United Kingdom.** David Utting. 1997.

162   **Imprisoned women and mothers.** Dianne Caddle and Debbie Crisp. 1996.

163.   **Curfew orders with electronic monitoring: an evaluation of the first twelve months of the trials in Greater Manchester, Norfolk and Berkshire, 1995 - 1996.** George Mair and Ed Mortimer. 1996..

164   **Safer cities and domestic burglaries.** Paul Ekblom, Ho Law, Mike Sutton, with assistance from Paul Crisp and Richard Wiggins. 1996.

165.   **Enforcing financial penalties.** Claire Whittaker and Alan Mackie. 1997.

166.   **Assessing offenders' needs: assessment scales for the probation service.** Rosumund Aubrey and Michael Hough. 1997.

167.   **Offenders on probation.** George Mair and Chris May. 1997.

168.   **Managing courts effectively: The reasons for adjournments in magistrates' courts.** Claire Whittaker, Alan Mackie, Ruth Lewis and Nicola Ponikiewski. 1997.

169.   **Addressing the literacy needs of offenders under probation supervision.** Gwynn Davis et al. 1997.

170.   **Understanding the sentencing of women.** edited by Carol Hedderman and Lorraine Gelsthorpe. 1997.

171.   **Changing offenders' attitudes and behaviour: what works?** Julie Vennard, Darren Sugg and Carol Hedderman 1997.

172   **Drug misuse declared in 1996: latest results from the British Crime Survey.** Malcolm Ramsay and Josephine Spiller. 1997.

No. 159 is not published yet.

Research Findings

30.   **To scare straight or educate? The British experience of day visits to prison for young people.** Charles Lloyd. 1996.

31.   **The ADT drug treatment programme at HMP Downview – a preliminary evaluation.** Elaine Player and Carol Martin. 1996.

32.   **Wolds remand prison – an evaluation.** Keith Bottomley, Adrian James, Emma Clare and Alison Liebling. 1996.

33. **Drug misuse declared: results of the 1994 British Crime Survey.** Malcolm Ramsay and Andrew Percy. 1996.

34. **Crack cocaine and drugs-crime careers.** Howard Parker and Tim Bottomley. 1996.

35. **Imprisonment for fine default.** David Moxon and Claire Whittaker. 1996.

36. **Fine impositions and enforcement following the Criminal Justice Act 1993.** Elizabeth Charman, Bryan Gibson, Terry Honess and Rod Morgan. 1996.

37. **Victimisation in prisons.** Ian O'Donnell and Kimmett Edgar. 1996.

38. **Mothers in prison.** Dianne Caddle and Debbie Crisp. 1997.

39. **Ethnic minorities, victimisation and racial harassment.** Marian Fitzgerald and Chris Hale. 1996.

40. **Evaluating joint performance management between the police and the Crown Prosecution Service.** Andrew Hooke, Jim Knox and David Portas. 1996.

41. **Public attitudes to drug-related crime**. Sharon Grace. 1996.

42. **Domestic burglary schemes in the safer cities programme**. Paul Ekblom, Ho Law and Mike Sutton. 1996.

43. **Pakistani women's experience of domestic violence in Great Britain.** Salma Choudry. 1996.

44. **Witnesses with learning disabilities**. Andrew Sanders, Jane Creaton, Sophia Bird and Leanne Weber. 1997.

45. **Does treating sex offenders reduce reoffending?** Carol Hedderman and Darren Sugg. 1996.

46. **Re-education programmes for violent men - an evaluation.** Russell Dobash, Rebecca Emerson Dobash, Kate Cavanagh and Ruth Lewis. 1996.

47. **Sentencing without a pre-sentence report**. Nigel Charles, Claire Whittaker and Caroline Ball. 1997.

48. **Magistrates' views of the probation service.** Chris May. 1997.

49.   **PACE ten years on: a review of the research.** David Brown. 1997.

50   **Persistent drug–misusing offenders.** Malcolm Ramsay. 1997.

51   **Curfew orders with electronic monitoring: The first twelve months.** Ed Mortimer and George Mair. 1997.

52   **Police cautioning in the 1990s.** Roger Evans and Rachel Ellis. 1997.

53.   **A reconviction study of HMP Grendon Therapeutic Community.** Peter Marshall. 1997.

54.   **Control in category c prisons.** Simon Marshall. 1997.

55.   **The prevalence of convictions for sexual offending.** Peter Marshall. 1997.

56   **Drug misuse declared in 1996: key results from the British Crime Survey.** Malcolm Ramsay and Josephine Spiller. 1997.

57   **The 1996 International Crime Victimisation Survey.** Pat Mayhew and Phillip White. 1997.

58   **The sentencing of women: a section 95 publication.** Carol Hedderman and Lizanne Dowds. 1997.

Occasional Papers

Mental disorder in remand prisoners. Anthony Maden, Caecilia J. A. Taylor, Deborah Brooke and John Gunn. 1996.

An evaluation of prison work and training. Frances Simon and Claire Corbett. 1996.

The impact of the national lottery on the horse-race betting levy. Simon Field. 1996.

Evaluation of a Home Office initiative to help offenders into employment. Ken Roberts, Alana Barton, Julian Buchanan, and Barry Goldson. 1997.

The impact of the national lottery on the horse-race betting levy.

Simon Field and James Dunmore. 1997.

Requests for Publications

Home Office Research Studies from 143 onwards, *Research and Planning Unit Papers, Research Findings and Research Bulletins* can be requested, **subject to availability**, from:

Research and Statistics Directorate
Information and Publications Group
Room 201, Home Office
50 Queen Anne's Gate
London SW1H 9AT
Telephone: 0171-273 2084
Fascimile: 0171-222 0211
Internet: http://www.open.gov.uk/home_off/rsd/rsdhome.htm
E-mail: rsd.ha apollo @ gtnet.gov.u.

Occasional Papers can be purchased from:
Home Office
Publications Unit
50 Queen Anne's Gate
London SW1H 9AT
Telephone: 0171 273 2302

Home Office Research Studies prior to 143 can be purchased from:

HMSO Publications Centre

(Mail, fax and telephone orders only)
PO Box 276, London SW8 5DT
Telephone orders: 0171-873 9090
General enquiries: 0171-873 0011
(queuing system in operation for both numbers)
Fax orders: 0171-873 8200

*And also from **HMSO Bookshops***